Mary E. Reid

W9-BGR-192

The Korea *Story*

*To the missionary men and women of all faiths,
who by their work and by their lives have laid
the foundations for true democracy in the Far East*

The Korea *Story*

John C. Caldwell

In collaboration with LESLEY FROST

HENRY REGNERY COMPANY

Chicago · 1952

Copyright 1952

HENRY REGNERY COMPANY, *Chicago, Illinois*

Manufactured in the United States of America

Foreword

FOR MANY MONTHS generals and lesser officers, noncoms, and privates have been returning to the United States to teach our troops in training the lessons to be learned from the war in Korea. These have been valuable lessons, learned at a frightful cost in blood and suffering. Old concepts of warfare and training and supposedly good weapons have been scrapped. In Korea our men have learned again to fight a guerilla warfare; they have learned that to defeat communism in battle it is often necessary to fight in the hills and mountains where jeeps and tanks cannot venture.

The story of the war and of the military lessons we have learned has been told many times over. But there is another part of our Korea story that has not been told, and there are other lessons that have not yet been learned. It is this other part that I have attempted to tell. It is the story of events prior to that fateful Sunday in June when the communist armies stormed across the 38th Parallel. It is the story of our occupation of South Korea, our sponsorship of the first elections in a nation's history, and the work of the American Mission in Korea, the largest diplomatic establishment ever to be maintained overseas by our Department of State. It is a story of great opportunities not seized upon, of mistakes made and not corrected. The Korea story is in many respects an aftermath of our tragic mistakes in China.

It is not always possible to tell this story in chronological sequence. Events and personalities of one period must be related to our activities in other periods; mistakes made in Seoul, Chunchon, or Kaesong must be traced back to other mistakes made in Washington or Nanking. To tell the story it is necessary to write of men and women who did their jobs well and of others who failed, to describe isolated events and attitudes.

In a large measure, our Korea story is the story of the Department of State and how it operates. It is possible that my judgment of the men and the operations of this department is wrong at times, is perhaps prejudiced by my own belief in the fundamental goodness and possibilities that lie in the people of Korea and China and my further belief that these people have, with tragic consequences to ourselves, been betrayed.

The nonmilitary lessons to be learned from Korea are, I am convinced, every bit as important as the military lessons, and this importance will not be changed by the outcome of the truce talks, still in progress as this is being written. An old Korean proverb tells us, "You can mend with a trowel today what it will take a spade to mend tomorrow." Already the day of the trowel is behind us.

Nashville   J. C. C.
August 1, 1952

TABLE OF CONTENTS

LIST OF ILLUSTRATIONS

Our Chronology in Korea

THE FOLLOWING TIMETABLE of American participation in Korean affairs may be helpful. American interest in Korea was expressed in the Cairo Declaration of December 1, 1943, which affirmed that "in due course Korea shall become free and independent." Actually, American intervention in Korean affairs came about as a result of the Yalta and Potsdam conferences.

September 8, 1945—American troops landed at Inchon to begin occupation (Russian troops entered Korea two weeks earlier and had pushed south of the 38th Parallel into the cities of Kaesong and Chunchon in order to loot before the Americans arrived).

US-USSR Joint Commission on Korea met throughout 1946–47 to seek a solution to the problem of Korean independence.

United Nations Temporary Commission on Korea, appointed after breakdown of US-USSR talks, arrived in Seoul in January 1948. After Russians refused entry into North Korea, the U.N. ordered elections in the southern zone.

First Korean elections, UN-supervised, held on May 10, 1948.

National assembly, elected as result of the voting, met in June and July to draft constitution and to elect Dr. Syngman Rhee as first president.

Republic of Korea proclaimed August 15, 1948. Rhee inaugurated; General John R. Hodge left. John J. Muccio arrived as special representative of President Truman; American troops began withdrawal; military government ended; Department of State began take-over of responsibility from U. S. Army.

January 1, 1949—American Mission in Korea (State Department) officially took over all American activities in Korea.

June 29, 1949—The last 7,500 American troops were withdrawn leaving behind a 500-man Military Advisory Group under direction of the ambassador.

May 30, 1950—Second Korean elections.

June 25, 1950—North Korean invasion began.

June 26, 27, 28—Americans evacuated to Japan.

June 27—American planes thrown into support of Republic of Korea troops.

June 29—American ground troops committed.

The Korea *Story*

Chapter I

Peacock Mountain

CHUNCHON, where my Korea story begins, is a small town not far from the 38th Parallel. There are two roads, one short, one long, leading north to the Parallel. These were immediately named Short Russia and Long Russia by the GI's of our Military Occupation stationed there. In months to come, the Chinese "volunteers" were to pour over these roads in their last ill-fated spring offensive of 1951. Two and three years later there were to be bloody battles fought near by, at Wonju, the Hwachon reservoir, Bloody-nose Ridge. Chunchon has figured often in the past two years in our official communiqués and has long since been wiped out according to the Air Force.

When I went there in the winter of 1948, Chunchon was one of the loveliest of Korean cities, the most beautiful part of it being the shrine on the side of Peacock Mountain, which rises a thousand feet from the center of the city like the pistil at the heart of a flower. It was to be the romantic background for courting my future wife, Elsie Fletcher, whose parents, Dr. and Mrs. A. G. Fletcher, had long been missionaries in Korea. Elsie had been born and bred there, spoke the language like a native, and was beloved by the people. As it turned out, she was to be my assistant in the information work to which I had been assigned as a civilian information specialist of the American Army of Occupation.

It was January, and bitterly cold, when I arrived in Seoul's massive railway station in the early morning. I was bundled to the teeth in a heavy parka, but even so I was chilled to the marrow of my bones. I was met by two friends who were to accompany me on my mission to Chunchon and was immediately transferred to another conveyance which was awaiting us. This odd-looking affair, commonly called the "doodlebug" by the GI's, was a single gasoline rail car divided into two sections, the forward half being for Americans and the rear for Koreans. The front section was outfitted with a small wood stove. The Korean passengers had no such luxury. Not that the stove helped greatly, since every window leaked air like a sieve; but we would have felt more comfortable if the Koreans had been able to share what little heat there was. I had a horrid suspicion that the Americans were perhaps adopting customs laid down by the Japanese or, even worse, setting up distinctions of their own, and that it could not but hurt us in a nation so recently liberated. I looked on ashamed as our burly GI train guard forcibly ejected two Koreans who came into the "de luxe" section, perhaps by mistake.

As we zigzagged round the hills and through the innumerable tunnels and came within view of the lovely valley in which the city lay, I was startled by the beauty of the landscape—startled, and stirred with anticipation. What a perfect spot in which to live and work, into which to carry the story of the United States, in which to help Korea build a fine democracy of its own. The evil effects of the unnatural and totally unrealistic division of the country at the 38th Parallel might even be partially surmounted by our efforts.

The base for our operations in Kangwon Province was to be a magnificent Shinto shrine which was already being converted into a Korean library for the citizens of Chunchon. It stood high among the pines on the slopes of Peacock Mountain. We caught glimpses of its bright-red lacquered pillars and dull-red roof tiles as we approached by jeep from the Military Government headquarters where we had been taken from the railroad station for rest and food. It seemed to me that nothing could be more incongruous, more confused by strange contrasts, than to be organizing an American information office in a Japanese shrine in the Korean hinterland. When we came to the shrine itself, we were spellbound by its romantic beauty and were reminded that we were here not only to impart information and make it come alive but also to establish this American outpost as a symbol of the meeting of two great cultures, one young, one old.

I learned afterwards that the Koreans were somewhat fearful we might be treading with too little understanding and respect upon something peculiarly their own. They consider Peacock Mountain sacred. The memory of the day in Kaesong, not long before, when GI's practicing with a bulldozer had wrecked much of the remains of the Koryo Dynasty palace, was still with the elders. However, they were somewhat reassured by an omen. The story goes that when the Japanese were building the shrine, a spirit (incognito as a tiger!) had carried away the priests at night. This same tiger (only he turned out to be a leopard when we found his tracks next morning!) had come to our own door over the moonlit snow. Then he had retraced his steps and gone away into the forests. The tiger had discovered we were Americans, not Japanese. We were established!

Handsome as it was, there was nothing utilitarian or functional about the architecture, equipment, or location of our new American information center in Korea. The shrine was halfway up a mountain, reached by a flight of three hundred steps from the Provincial Government buildings. We had no more than arrived when a blizzard swept in from the Diamond Mountains, the temperature fell below zero, and it took a squad of workers working continuously to keep the steps clear for the delivery of books, furniture, and motion-picture equipment. If stoves could have been obtained (which they could not) they would scarcely have been felt in the cold of the high drafty halls. We worked furiously to keep from freezing and to be ready for our official opening scheduled for February 14. The Military Governor, Major General William Dean (the same General Dean who was later wounded at the battle of Taejon, awarded our nation's highest military honor, and lost and finally located in a communist prison camp), was expected to fly in for the occasion, but another snowfall obliterated the tiny airstrip, and the general never arrived.

However, we went ahead with the ceremonies, and we felt warm in spirit if not in body. We were the forerunners in a thrilling undertaking—the more difficult and hazardous, the more thrilling! We were part of the United States Army Office of Civil Information, the part thrust forward closest to the Parallel. What Korea would know of America rested on our shoulders. So many would owe so much to so few (there were seventeen of us at that time in all South Korea), and to so little in the way of equipment. It would be our spirit mainly that would overcome all obstacles. Some of us had enthusiasm to spare in the early days.

Our two-thousand-volume American library (alas, the Washington planners had taken the Korean's lack of English into small account) was set up in the great hall. We had a magazine room, a small theatre, and rooms for record concerts, forum discussions, and English classes.

The wave of the future in Chunchon was unquestionably the desire to know English and so to learn about democracy —perhaps some day to go to America. Classes were quickly arranged for students, business and professional men, housewives, and teachers. Our hope was not so much to teach English. The Japanese had forced all Koreans to study Japanese, and we did not wish to set up any grounds for odious comparison. But through the English classes we hoped to encourage talk, discussion, and argument about the true meaning of that magic word *democracy* and the approaches to self-government.

Our first serious contretemps occurred when we attempted to hold mixed classes, thinking to break the strict laws of the former Japanese administration against coeducation, and also feeling that such an old American custom would bear export. We were wrong on both counts. On the orders of parents and teachers alike, classes went out on strike. It took the combined diplomatic maneuvers of the staff, assisted by Lieutenant Fred Mueller, the Military Government education advisor, to bring about a compromise. Both sides backtracked. The students returned to their classes, but boys and girls came at staggered hours in order not to meet except in passing. And we learned that some things that appeared good to us could not be pushed too fast.

In every way, particularly during the first months, the physical handicaps were almost insuperable. During the remainder of the winter we nearly perished of the cold. It all but paralyzed our movements. It brought our jeep to a practical standstill. After we had spent hours starting it, we invariably wound up a short sweet run stalled in a snowdrift. Even when the road to Seoul was temporarily and miraculously cleared, it was next to impossible to obtain the day-to-day supplies necessary for keeping our program alive and kicking.

The telephone was another roadblock! As in combat, the Army set up exchanges with code names. Ours was Whitehorse. Every call in or out resulted in a major battle, and the battle in a dismal defeat. Victory went to the Koreans, who expertly cut in on the better maintained American lines and jammed us with a chorus of gay remarks and endless conversations; or to the operators, who connected us with Taegu when we wanted Seoul, or Pusan when we asked for Kaesong. The climax came one day when I found myself talking to MacArthur's headquarters in Japan!

As for electric power, it was even more off-again-on-again Finnigan. We undressed by candlelight. Reading after sundown was never practiced enough to become a fixed habit. Then, in May, the Russians turned off the power completely (the plants feeding electricity to Kangwon Province were north of the Parallel on the Hwachon reservoir) in retaliation against the success of the first South Korean elections.

There was no current for weeks. For heating our rooms we resorted to diesel-oil camp stoves, and the stoves alternately exploded in clouds of greasy black soot or froze solid due to water in the oil. No wonder, at times like these, that tempers were short and that even the Americans in Chunchon, at the almost forgotten end of a long supply line, sometimes found themselves at odds with each other.

Moreover, there were too few of us at Chunchon to be really effective, and, unfortunately, even what we did was done according to regulations set up for dealing with a vanquished country rather than a liberated one. The 100th Military Government Group, of which we were a part, consisted of ten officers and seven civilians, with a number of enlisted men to look after the dirty work. We were minute compared to the teeming populace of Korea. This made our work supremely challenging from the psychological as well as physical standpoint. For, while the general climate of opinion in Korea was favorable to the United States, the Occupation had made several serious mistakes which the Communists had eagerly seized upon and were exploiting at a great rate.

For one thing, we had allowed the Japanese police system to be maintained. The ranking officers of the police force were largely Japanese-trained Koreans who knew only Japanese methods and Japanese ideas of what constitutes justice and humanity toward a subject people. Since many of the American police advisors (there was one in each province and a group of them in Seoul) were themselves convinced through race prejudice, ignorance, and lack of education in national differences that the "gooks" only understood force, it was difficult to uphold the dignity of the United States, let alone the dignity of man, among the people at large.

I recall a peculiarly painful incident which occurred shortly after our arrival in Chunchon. A schoolhouse having been destroyed by arson, the police arrested the entire teaching staff and tortured each of its members for several days in an attempt to gain a confession of guilt. A half-witted boy finally admitted the crime. Nothing about the affair could be said to reflect honor on the Americans who were there, it was claimed, to promote justice. There were other incidents, less tragic but nevertheless indicating our failure to understand the land and its people. It was a serious and even a deadly failure, for it doubtless made numbers of Koreans easy victims of the communist "cursed hebona" poured into the ear.

A further psychological factor, which threw a monkeywrench into the American spokes in Korea was the tense situation with regard to communist infiltration from the North. This had, by 1948, already reached a critical condition, with fear and hate apparent among the people and in the government. The latter was adopting vigorous measures, and well it might, to keep the Communists down and out. The South Korean Labor Party, bossed from the North, had been driven underground. But in its zeal to destroy the enemy, the government often cracked down on the rights of innocent people. People were executed with less and less attempt at a fair trial. There was increasingly little true freedom of expression or action.

For the American Occupation it was a situation which demanded great wisdom and experience, and we were lacking in both. The dilemma was one that few but the hard-hearted could face: Was it better to tolerate a suspected communist employee or friend or to turn him in, merely on suspicion, to be a victim of the most intolerable brutality? He was seldom turned in.

Furthermore, American operations were made difficult by the lack of trained or intelligent personnel. The average American, whether officer, private, or civilian, disliked Korea and the Koreans. He kept aloof from both and spent his time at his office, canteen, or club. In his work, the American was often totally out of his element. When an Army lieutenant who has never finished high school is assigned the post of educational advisor for a whole province, and an Air Force lieutenant is appointed manager of a large and important silk mill on the outskirts of Chunchon, it is quite possible that school and silk mill alike will not be particularly grateful. Such men, irrespective of what "nice fellows" they were at the club, were scarcely aware of what was needed for the political, economic, and spiritual regeneration of Korea.

Still another hurdle, a most disastrous one, in the path of American policy and usefulness in Korea, was the division at the 38th Parallel. Whoever thought up the idea in the first place committed a crime against a small, helpless nation, the kind of crime committed only by large powers riding rough-shod over minorities. Korea is a distinct and homogeneous body from the Yalu River south. There is no more differ-ence, ethnologically speaking, between the residents of Seoul or Pusan in the south and Pyongyang in the north than there is between the people of Baltimore and Nashville. Language and customs are the same. Yet the 38th not only cut a nation in two; it divided property, transportation, and economy. Most terrible of all, it tore families apart. It was difficult for those living in one sector to communicate with relatives in the other. Parents and children were separated, marriages dis-rupted; the strongly-knit pattern of Korean family life was broken.

While attempting to explain the behavior of Koreans, we gave far too little attention to what they had experienced under forty years of Japanese occupation. The twig had been bent and could scarcely be expected to straighten overnight. From absolute tyranny the people suddenly found them-selves technically free, supposedly with no strings attached. Freedom was a heady brew. Thousands of Koreans believed themselves to be chosen to lead their nation out of travail. Between 1945 and 1947, nearly two hundred political parties and social groups emerged, each with a magic formula for bringing social and economic stability. At times the "politi-cal party," perhaps bearing some such typically Korean name as the Full Moon Meeting Society, might be only one man and his family group.

Under the Japanese rule, it had been all but impossible for

a Korean to attain to a responsible position in government, or outside it, for that matter. Actually, things were little better after liberation; yet each man was free to make himself heard. Now and then someone "arrived," but it was more by chance than ability. Nor was it easy to throw off the habits of a lifetime. The populace had learned, the hard way, that it paid to malinger on the job, to be late to work, steal, lie, and carry on a constant hit-and-run strategy against the alien overlord. Fundamentally, we Americans were liked, but a new morality could not be expected to reappear quickly, even under American tutelage—which often did not set the best of examples either.

Then there was the refugee problem to further complicate the problems of the Military Government. Soon after the communist regime had been thoroughly established north of the Parallel, thousands of Koreans picked up their beds and walked southward. There were no barbed wire barriers to stop them, nothing more difficult than the rivers and mountain passes they were familiar with. The Parallel crossed through farms, villages, and cities, and those on the northern side soon decided to move over to the southern, as Germans have done in Berlin. The Korean peasant may be politically naïve, but as the communist government grew more tyrannical, the flow of refugees steadily increased, until there were more than two million.

South Korea's population density being second only to India's, these refugees became a physical and psychological handicap to the democratic processes of government. Flowing into the interstices of an already overcrowded economy, they seriously threatened its functioning. Yet the migration was a natural one, and nothing would have been more cruel than to repulse these unhappy people behind the phony 38th; as it would now be equally cruel and unforgivable to return unwilling prisoners of war to death and torture. Every night for nearly five years the white-clad hordes poured through the mountain passes along the Short and Long Russia roads. As tired GI's were to find out many months later, it was impossible to separate the genuine refugees from the spies, the saboteurs, and the troublemakers, who fanned out into all of South Korea to wait for the signal from the North.

Last, but not least, the issue of collaboration with the Japanese was everywhere a wellspring of serious trouble. Who, in the dark years of the Japanese occupation, had been a collaborator?—who a patriot? Thousands upon thousands had to work for the Japanese or starve. Consequently, the moment peace was declared, a national argument began. Koreans were even encouraged to inform on their neighbors and erstwhile friends. Boxes, like mail boxes, stood on street corners, and a collaborator could be denounced merely by sticking his name through the slot. This appeal made mincemeat out of family, church, and business affiliations.

To cap the climax, it was against American military regulations to eat Korean food, visit Korean restaurants or homes, or stay at Korean hotels. It was contrary to orders to invite Koreans to one's own mess or billet or to an American club. This meant that Americans could go scarcely anywhere outside the cities to which they were assigned, even had they wanted to—which they didn't! It meant that any friendly relationship between American and Korean was pretty thoroughly dried up at the source. It meant that our penetration of Korea was singularly shallow and had little hope of going deeper. Unfortunately, American-Korean relationships during the years of Military Government were those of masters and servants, of a subject people taking orders rather than friends taking advice, of an inferior race being socially condescended to by foreign officialdom.

Add to the above tensions the tangle of red tape produced by our own Military Government rules and regulations, the lack of coordination between military and civilian personnel, the human weaknesses we all are heir to, and the frustrating effect of Washington's merry-go-round on the local bureaucracy, and you have a situation that was well-nigh insoluble. Yet there were opportunities, great opportunities, for those with initiative. With all of its confusions, we could fight communism under the Occupation, as we were to find we could not under the State Department.

Most of us in those days were unbelievably naïve about the 38th Parallel and the darkness that lay beyond it. We were too busy trying to keep warm and find our way through the workings of the military. There were those who warned of danger, and Lieutenant General John R. Hodge, Commanding General of the American forces in Korea, was one of these. I remember that during the winter of '48 a young intelligence captain came from Hodge's office to talk to us in Chunchon about the danger of an eventual attack from the North. He had been assigned to visit similar outposts throughout South Korea. He told of the close proximity of Russian airfields, or of this division and that division in the North.

Fresh from the atmosphere of Washington, less than a year removed from an assignment with the Marshall mission in China, this talk of the menace of communism was indeed strange, almost shocking, to my ears. But General Hodge became a victim of the times. Washington thought he was too hard on the Communists. The realistic Korean leaders thought he was not hard enough.

This was the Korea of the winter of 1948, when I chugged up the side of Peacock Mountain and entered the Shinto shrine with hope for the future of Korea. My territory extended north to the Parallel, then seventy-five miles eastward as the crow flies, to the Sea of Japan, thence nearly one hundred miles southward into the wild mountain mass below Wonju and Yongwol. I felt then, and feel today, that if our American aims and ideals could be firmly and intelligently enough presented to the Koreans, or any other people, and if, at the same time, we attempted to understand the culture and inherent nature of lands strange to us, we could build a firm foundation for international cooperation.

Chapter 2

Liberators and Liberated

FACING the job of setting up an information program in Chunchon, and of making it somehow effective, I took careful stock of myself and the people with whom I was to work. Even though I had been born of missionary parents in next-door China and had during World War II worked behind Japanese lines in that country, I knew as little about Korea as did most Americans in 1948. That was very little!

Before leaving Washington for Korea I read what I could lay hands on and remember that I was impressed by the descriptions of the Korean climate. The encyclopedia went so far in its praise as to call it "salubrious." I also recall checking with a Foreign Service officer in the Department of State and of learning from him the interesting though hardly important fact that all Koreans wore white clothing because in ancient times it had been customary to wear white during the long mourning periods following the death of Korean kings. Few of these early kings were permitted to live their full lives, with the result that over a period of several hundred years the people became accustomed to a state of mourning and white was gradually adopted as the national color.

I had assumed, I fear, as many Americans still do, that Koreans closely resemble the Chinese, or perhaps the Japanese. As a matter of fact, this is not true in any important sense. Korea has a culture completely its own and a history which began some four thousand three hundred years ago. The Korean language is a distinct language, related to Chinese only in that there are many derivative words (somewhat as many English words are derived from Latin) resulting from the centuries in which Korea suffered Chinese domination.

In some instances this relation has brought about a strange duality of language. There are two systems of counting, for example: Korean and Chinese. In telling time the Korean word is used for the hour, the Chinese for the minute. The Korean language is difficult and highly grammatical, while Chinese is almost lacking in grammar and is extremely tonal in character. The Chinese language is rich in blasphemy and obscenity, and I was surprised to find the Korean language remarkably pure. The reason soon became apparent. There are three types of verb endings in Korean, known as high talk, middle talk, and low talk. A man addresses dogs, his children, and his wife in low talk; the wife, however, must use high talk in speaking to her husband. The hair-raising curses of the Chinese are therefore not necessary. The same effect can be achieved by using low talk where high or middle talk would be customary. Many a Korean has been put in his place by the intentional misuse of a verb ending.

Among the well educated, the written language is a mixture of Chinese and the Korean phonetic script. In addition, the Koreans can and do use their own written language known as Hangul. Hangul is based upon a simple alphabet of twenty-four letters which are very easily learned and are so arranged that every word is written exactly as it sounds. Soon after the war ended, a large-scale adult education program was started with the primary objective of teaching Hangul to the thousands who under the Japanese rule had had no opportunity to learn it. Hand in hand with the study of Hangul simple newspapers and magazines were developed so that there would be reading material for those who spoke the language. It was all a part of being liberated, since the Japanese had forbidden the teaching of Hangul. Even the spoken word in Korean had been so frowned upon that it was only used in the privacy of the home.

Korean food, living customs, recreation, all differ essentially from those of the Chinese and Japanese. Several centuries ago the Koreans discovered a method of radiant heating, and their manner of living is largely dependent upon it. A small aperture, or fireplace, is built into the foundations of the houses, with flues running under the floor to the chimney on the opposite wall. The floor is made of flat rocks and plaster, with a carpeting of heavy oiled paper. A fire built in the foundation fireplace heats the floor as the smoke and flames circulate through the flues sucked toward the chimney by the natural drafts. One fire a day is usually all that is required since the floor, once heated, will stay hot for hours. It is easy to see, therefore, that this type of heating, universally used from the Yalu to Pusan, more or less dictates the daily routine of living. The floor being the one warm place, the family sleeps on the floor, sits on the floor, eats on the floor. Beds, tables, and chairs are unnecessary.

Because the oil-paper floor covering is easily worn, shoes are always removed before one enters a Korean home. The shoe-removing habit is automatic. It is even done before entering the place of business, the school, the office. It is done so often that the Korean carries a shoehorn with him as we might carry a pocket comb. The custom has its roots in good housekeeping and good economy as well as in courtesy. Yet many Americans, not understanding its purpose, would not take the trouble to "unshoe." To Americans it was inconvenient and uncomfortable (particularly in the dead of winter!), but it is a part of Korean etiquette which cannot be overlooked.

In the production of art objects and curios so dear to the American's heart, the Koreans are far behind their Chinese and Japanese neighbors. This can be blamed on history to a great extent: weak kings; external pressure from China, Russia, Japan; and, lastly, the long period of Japanese occupation. The Korean temples and monasteries are beautiful but do not match those of China in grandeur. The ancient palaces are interesting but cannot be compared to those of Peiping.

The modest Korean makes relatively little that the American tourist will buy. It is not that such things cannot be made or never were made. There was a period in Korean history, not too long ago, when Korean porcelain was unmatched in beauty and was widely copied by the artisans of China and Japan. The magnificent brass-bound chests of two and three hundred years ago are unsurpassed in workmanship. The modern brass-makers of Korea are still among the most famous in the Orient.

Even though the Korean at present lacks the cultural richness of his neighbors, though he has lived more primitively and built less stately temples, he has a tremendous vitality, a wondrous sense of humor, and a great willingness to learn. Perhaps his vitality is best expressed in his beautiful, haunting folk music with which most Americans fall in love. Every Korean sings, and he sings without restraint, from his innermost being. Following Korean dinners or feasts, it is expected that every guest will sing a song, solo. And the American guest must do likewise. My embarrassment was considerable, since I can never remember the words to even the most popular American tune! I soon developed a method to get by. I sang a song in my native Foochow Chinese dialect, a dialect no Korean could understand.

It is perhaps indicative of the tragic current of Korean history that most of the songs are laments of lovers separated, of grief and yearning. Dancing and singing are intimately linked together. During Korean festivals, whole villages turn out for the dancing, which is done singly (as with the singing) and with the emphasis on movements of the upper part of the body, particularly the shoulders. With a little rice wine to help them, the men enjoy the dancing as much as the women.

In handling my Korean staff, I soon found that this rice wine, or any alcohol, was a problem I never had to contend with among my Chinese employees. Koreans do not drink much, but they are easily affected by the little they do drink.

Rice wine, or *sool*, is weak in alcoholic content, but it doesn't take much of it to upset the equilibrium of a Korean. I could easily comprehend why it was that the early missionaries had strenuously opposed drinking. Unfortunately, the Americans in Korea failed to provide a good example in this respect, and whiskey is far too potent for Koreans in general. The well-organized rings of Korean petty thieves used the American drinking orgies to advantage. A houseboy or housegirl would send word to the gang when a big party was scheduled, and a raid would take place in the wee hours when the Americans were far from alert.

I had always found the Chinese easy to work with. I assumed the Koreans would be equally so. I was mistaken. However, the difficulties I did encounter in this respect were so much a part of the Koreans' recent humiliating struggle with their Japanese conquerors that I found something challenging, even fascinating, in trying to establish a good working relationship with them. The centuries-old position Korea has occupied as a cat's-paw in power politics, the forty years of brutal Japanese rule, and the sudden liberation that yet brought with it the terrible experience of being cut clean through the middle and left standing, all contributed to a certain mass, and individual, psychopathic condition. It made these normally intelligent, humorous, honest people behave in unpredictable ways that drew severe criticism from the Americans. It only went to prove again that an occupied country is a sad affair at best, only a twisted makeshift of itself.

Though, as I have said, the Korean is fundamentally able and intelligent, he had been deprived for so many years of all positions of respect and responsibility that he was totally out of practice (under the Japanese 67 per cent of all teaching positions in colleges and universities, including all the top jobs, were held by Japanese). It was extremely hard to find qualified persons for the many government jobs suddenly opened to them under our Military Government. General Hodge tried to give as much authority to the Koreans as possible, believing that only through experience, trial, and error could they learn to stand on their own feet. By 1948 he had already made changes that were designed to answer the Korean protests against being "ruled" by Americans. Military governors in the provinces were to be called civil affairs officers. The directors of the various national and provincial departments were called advisors. But the name doesn't make the article. In name, a Korean was, for instance, director of education in Kangwon Province, with an American as advisor. Actually, in nine cases out of ten, the advisors ran the show even to tacking their signatures onto every important document.

It was not only difficult to find trained and responsible employees; because of the collaboration issue, mentioned earlier, it was also difficult to find employees who worked well together. The 38th Parallel, the years of Japanese rule, the increasing communist pressure, all contributed to our headaches in this respect.

In the 1940's, the Japanese had ordered all Koreans to visit the Shinto shrines once a month, there to bow before a spirit of the Emperor and pray for victory. A large number of Christians, some of them with the support of their missionary advisors, resolutely refused to bow down before a "graven image" in violation of Biblical teachings. Other leaders, including some of the most respected Christians, advised their followers to obey orders, since the act could be committed tongue in cheek, so to speak. But still, hundreds of Christians were imprisoned and brutally tortured because of the edict.

As soon as World War II was over, a new war began within the Church on just this issue. The non-bowers felt, perhaps with justification, that their patriotism and religious fervor had proved itself superior to that of the bowers. Congregations fell out among themselves, and to this day the wounds have not healed. Indeed, the same kind of cruel question has now arisen among the North Koreans: who is the better

Christian and patriot, he who stayed on in the North and made the best of things under the Communists; or he who fought back and was imprisoned, or worse; or he who fled to the South and joined with the Americans, throwing himself on our mercies and protection? It is a question in which we are deeply involved. Along with a political and military commitment, we also assumed a moral one which urgently demands a solution. The solution, however difficult to find, must be reached not only with justice but with simple humanity as well.

As for the two million or more refugees from the North who did join us, they created an enormous social and psychological problem, and still do. Often the Northerner was more aggressive, better trained, or better educated than his Southern cousin. There were certainly not enough jobs to go around, and in the scramble for employment the North Korean "alien" (only because the Parallel made him one) often came out the winner. There is, to repeat, no real difference between the North and the South Koreans, but friction and controversy were bound to develop under the fearful economic strains put upon the South. The patriotic North Korean felt that since he had had the gumption to pick up and leave the North, he was at least due some recognition in the shape of the opportunity to make a living. The result was that in most large organizations people split into two factions. The situation was far from conducive to good morale and efficient work.

I have mentioned the great difficulty of discovering who among the refugees was a Communist. Even here in America, during the past few years, we have learned that it is all but impossible to identify the infiltrator. Imagine, then, the difficulty of weeding out the enemy in a country as strange to us as Korea. The Army had no prearranged measuring stick. Indeed, investigation was utterly out of the question since there were no possible investigators to check the references. Who could check the investigators? It meant that anyone handling employment of Koreans had to rely entirely on his ability to judge character.

Yet the Department of State, which took over in 1949, instituted the type of security check used by the FBI in this country. Each job applicant had to fill out a long form listing all places of residence, all jobs, names of supervisors, employers, etc., covering a period of ten years. The whole thing was pure farce. It naturally never trapped a single Communist. But, worse still, it further confused the minds of the already thrice-bewildered Koreans.

During our months in Chunchon, and later during our two years in Seoul, my wife and I employed several hundred Koreans. Many were from the North. We have lately been able to go over our records carefully, and we have found that none among those we hired for important positions turned out to be a Communist. Amongst the rank and file, however, we made our share of mistakes. For instance, we have been able to completely check a unit of ten whom we employed in the visuals section of the U. S. information center in Seoul, a section long supervised by Elsie. Of these ten, five were sufficiently loyal to join the tide of refugees who moved south out of Seoul in June and July of 1950. The chief of the section, a fine artist by the name of Kim Soon Bok (Slim Kim), walked the 280 miles to Pusan and is still employed by the American Embassy.

Of the five who stayed, on the other hand, one has turned out to be a relatively important Communist, a district leader in Seoul, and the four others remaining in Seoul were weak enough to work for the communist regime in its propaganda offices. Slim Kim writes us from Pusan that none of the four are Communists. "For family reasons," he says, "they could not leave Seoul. They had to eat." Perhaps Slim is right, perhaps not, but I am inclined to believe him. Under such conditions, what one of us dares pronounce who is sinner and who isn't, what makes a collaborator and what makes a patriot? Certainly the involved State Department personnel forms will never give us the answers. Nor could we, who were doing our utmost to assemble a competent staff as quickly as possible in the winter of 1948 in Chunchon, hope to always guess correctly.

But we were unbelievably fortunate. The man I chose as my Korean codirector of the center proved to be one of the best, a truly good man dedicated to the fight ahead. He was Mr. Hong Shin, a South Korean Methodist minister who had traveled much in the North. Though rather insignificant-looking and seeming to hide behind dark glasses day and night, Mr. Hong proved to be a firebrand orator, completely fearless, and even more opposed to communism than he had been to the Japanese. It was several months before I discovered that the dark glasses were worn to conceal the loss of an eye in a brutal police beating. Mr. Hong had been a non-bowing Christian and had spent long months in Japanese prisons in consequence.

The man I picked for our chief assistant was Pak Chung Young. He was from the most northern, most communist section of North Korea. He had stayed on for a short time and had even served as a communist official. But when the communist authorities sent him to a special training school for *gun-sus*—that is, county commissioners—in Pyongyang, he had his eyes opened. He simply couldn't swallow what he learned, particularly the anti-Christian teachings. Eventually he deserted, slipped back to his home, gathered his wife and six children, and walked south. Because of his background he was continually being investigated, either by the South Korean police or by our own Counter Intelligence Corps. He was to prove himself one of the most stalwart patriots and prodemocrats we had in our employ.

Though these two men were far from being mental giants and had human failings, yet around them, and with their sincere help, we were able to build a small and devoted staff. But, closely associated with this problem of judging employees, arose still another difficulty. The United States Army had set up a rigid pay schedule for Koreans, with a minimum of 2,280 *won* a month and a maximum of 5,000. The *won* was officially pegged at fifty to the dollar, but in actual buying power it was much nearer two thousand to the dollar. On the official basis these salaries might have been adequate, but in practice the highest salary we could pay amounted to about $3.00 a month! One just could not employ well-educated honest men on that basis. Since it was completely impossible for a man with a family to survive on such a miserable stipend, the temptations to dishonesty were often beyond the strength of human flesh to resist, particularly since the opportunities were everywhere present.

Two other information centers had already been established in Korea before I opened the center at Chunchon, and from their American directors I learned certain tricks of the trade by which we could supplement the pay checks. For one: the Army permitted a certain amount of overtime, and the supervisors automatically added the maximum overtime whether it had been worked or not. For another: the payroll was padded each month with fictitious names, including signatures. Still another: the books from the information center library were sold on the black market. In other words, dishonesty became a part of the American habit also—even for the best of causes. A case for the end justifying the means, perhaps?

As for me, I found that American packing cases in which our books, projectors, and other equipment arrived, had tremendous value as lumber, the wood being far better than anything the average Korean could buy. I sold these for a good price, and the money went for extra salaries. Whenever a piece of equipment was considered unsalvageable (I always checked with Army to be safe), I sold that also. Since Elsie did not smoke, her cigarette ration, worth two thousand *won* per carton, was similarly added to the payroll "bank." We always tried to be as legitimate as possible. I believe it was because we were able to pay fairly decent wages that, in all our time at Chunchon, we only had one employee who stole from us.

I soon found, also, that most Americans in Korea operated entirely on the barter system, the official *won* exchange rate being such that few of us could afford to buy anything on the Korean markets. So there was a steady flow of cigarettes, toilet soap, candy bars, and gum into the Korean economy, in exchange for fresh fruit, fresh eggs, and the few curios and trinkets to be found. Anything American was worth a small fortune in Korean money, which resulted in a large number of black market operations, engaged in by men of all ranks. Tires, gasoline, and even jeeps joined the stream. I actually found it was far easier to get a needed jeep part on the Korean black market than from the Army itself, from which it had originated. The vastness of this operation, headed by Americans, is indicated by the fact that the Army reported two thousand jeeps missing in the course of a year! Periodically, the Korean police would hold a jeep roundup, parking dozens of vehicles on a parade ground while those of us who had lost jeeps would look them over, trying to find some distinguishing mark that would identify the vehicle. I had a jeep, locked with a heavy chain, stolen from in front of the Army PX in Seoul, but though I visited several roundups, I was never able to find it.

Yet, over and above all the afore-mentioned problems caused by Military Government red tape (many of the rules and regulations were never meant for Americans living and working in the lonely Korean mountains, ten thousand miles from Washington but only six miles from a deadly enemy plotting their downfall!), there was still another I could not have foreseen. I found that I also had to contend with a peculiar and maddening situation among my fellow Americans, upon whom I had to rely for logistic support, for advice, and for companionship. It seemed the American community of Chunchon, indeed of all Korean provincial capitals, was divided by its own little 38th!

The American troops landing at Inchon and Pusan in the fall of 1945 had a clear simple mission: to disarm and repatriate Japanese troops and Japanese civilians, and to establish, or assist in establishing, an independent Korean government. When it became obvious that the latter would be impossible, or at best a long-term job, a Military Government was superimposed on the Occupation forces. In each province there was a Military Government unit, but also a unit of tactical troops, generally in battalion strength, which came to be called Battalion for this reason. The Office of Civil Information, to which I belonged, was officially a part of the United States Armed Forces in Korea (USAFIK). Military Government was known as United States Military Government in Korea (USAMGIK) and in considerable part was made up of civilians. The latter's working relationships with the Koreans were much closer than that of the tactical units, while Military Government and Battalion were often poles apart.

Although a part of USAFIK, we in Chunchon lived and worked with Military Government. But we had to rely on Battalion for fuel, the extra vehicles we needed, our passes to the Parallel, our telephone service. But Military Government wasn't talking to Battalion! The split was positively ludicrous. It extended even into the social life of the few American wives in Chunchon, all living in a special compound at Battalion headquarters. Six of these were wives of Military Government officers. They had their own MG woman's club, and an MG bridge club, entirely apart from the Battalion wives with whom they resided. And even though it was a mere half mile between Military Government and Battalion, the chaplain was forced to conduct duplicate services on Sunday, first at Military Government and then at Battalion.

I was caught between the two camps. It required a good share of diplomacy and at times a certain double-dealing, to walk the tightrope stretched between the men I worked with and those who made the work possible. In this dilemma I was helped somewhat by the fact that Colonel James Gammon, the Military Governor, was a full colonel, while the various commanders who came and went at Battalion were always lieutenant colonels. The United States Army being what it is, the word of a full colonel carries considerable weight over lesser ranks, and I could always count on Colonel Gammon to stand by me when diplomacy failed.

In spite of the hurdles, our information center at Chunchon was ready and eager when we swung into full operation soon after our official opening on St. Valentine's Day of 1948. With the wise advice and ardent enthusiasm of Mr. Hong and Mr. Pak, and with Elsie's knowledge of the language and customs, we had gathered together a group of men anxious to help with the exciting and challenging work which lay in the immediate future: the planning and supervising of a democratic, secret election for two million people—people who had never voted before or even witnessed an election.

Chapter 3

The People Vote

TO UNDERSTAND the significance of the elections held in Korea in 1948, one must take a quick look at events leading up to them. Soon after the end of World War II, a US-USSR Joint Commission had been appointed and had met regularly in Seoul to try to solve the problem of the withdrawal of foreign troops and the creation of the independent Korea agreed upon by the Allies. The experience of this commission should certainly give us pause to wonder if any real results can be expected from the Kaesong-Panmunjun truce negotiations which have been dragging along for so many months now; for at that time, just as now, the Russians constantly brought up matters our negotiators had considered permanently decided, gummed up the works with inconsequential details, and bitterly attacked the West. It became apparent that the Russians did not want a real solution, that their talk of independence and democracy for Korea had no relation to our hopes.

Although the Russian liaison mission was still in Seoul when I arrived in Korea, General Hodge had given up some months before, and the United States had referred the Korean problem to the United Nations in the fall of 1947. The United Nations Commission on Korea was then created—over Russian objections, of course—and it arrived in Seoul in January 1948. For more than two long, tense years, the Korean people had hung suspended in a ghastly political vacuum while their fate had been wearisomely and fruitlessly discussed by the United States and Russia. Now the issues and the momentous possibilities were inherited by the United Nations Commission which, belatedly, had to seek a solution to the Korean problem created so ill-advisedly at Yalta and Potsdam.

On arrival, the commission sought permission to proceed north of the Parallel to inspect conditions prior to taking any action or making any recommendations. But here again we saw a preview of the present truce talks in which the Chinese and North Korean Communists have refused to allow even Red Cross units into the North. The Russians in 1948 promptly refused to let any of the commission members cross the border. At the time, we in Korea speculated what would happen if the commission showed some real gumption, got on a train and simply moved into North Korea on its own. One north–south train was still running. After all, the Russians could scarcely have afforded to shoot or capture the representatives of India, Canada, Australia, France, Syria, the Philippines, China and El Salvador! (The "independent" Ukrainian Soviet Socialist Republic had also been appointed to the commission, but had refused to fill the seat assigned to it.) The move could have been made but of course it wasn't.

Thereupon the commission announced its decision to hold an election in South Korea that would apply to the whole country. In other words, an election would be held in the American zone to establish a government that would, in time, have jurisdiction over Korea as a whole. A block of vacant seats would be held open in the national assembly-to-be until they could be filled by a free election in North Korea. This legal basis for South Korean claims of jurisdiction over all Korea, as well as moral obligations inherent in our promise to create a free, independent, and united Korea, seem to have been forgotten by some of our leaders who would consider a boundary settlement at or near the 38th Parallel as a victory.

Actually, of course, the proposed election was the responsibility of the United Nations rather than of the United

States. Our country was not even represented on the commission, but as far as the Koreans and most of the oriental world were concerned the United Nations was and is the United States.

General Hodge was determined to see that the election was free, honest, and a success in the eyes of the world as well as of the Korean people. For that reason he gave the Office of Civil Information (my organization) of the Occupation forces in Korea the responsibility of overseeing many aspects of the election. It was to be our top priority project. General Hodge alone, among top-ranking Occupation officials, believed the South Koreans capable of responding to the challenge of a democratic voting campaign. Since the time until election day was extremely short, military and civilian Americans alike were completely skeptical of the results. Impossible, they felt, for a nation which had never heard of electioneering or voting booths or multiple candidacies in its four thousand years of history, to cast ballots after a few weeks of propaganda.

We had less than a month to publicize the registration, and without an honest and heavy registration there could be no vote, or at least no honest and representative vote. To add to the difficulty, these weeks were torn by internal politics. Two of the country's most respected leaders, middle-of-the-road men, let it be known that they would boycott the whole undertaking. Many of their satellites followed suit. Those men, like some Americans today, like Prime Minister Nehru of India, believed in staying aloof in the hope that if we were patient and cooperative enough, the Communists would fall into step beside us and work with us. Some South Koreans feared that the proposed elections would turn the 38th Parallel into an irrevocable boundary line. If we waited, they argued, the communist authorities might change their minds and a unified democratic Korea might be formed with the participation of all factions.

Furthermore, from the day the elections were announced,

South Koreans were subjected to a continuous propaganda attack from the North. They were told that the elections were but a trick to consolidate the hold of the avaricious, imperialistic Americans and to put into power that stooge of the Americans, Syngman Rhee. This last argument was rather ludicrous, since Syngman Rhee and General Hodge had hardly been on speaking terms for months!

There was nothing to do but go ahead with our plans in spite of all opposition. It was too late to backtrack. The national and provincial election commissions had already been organized. The orders had gone out.

As consultant for the election commission of Kangwon Province I had the privilege of taking an inside part in every phase of the election strategy: the setting up of voting districts and electoral districts; the printing and distribution of the ballots; the safe conduct of ballot boxes and ballots into and from remote communities; insuring an honest count once the votes had been cast; and, most important of all, the dissemination of information and know-how.

From the first, we found the undertaking almost beyond human power to cope with. The ballots (and this was something we hadn't thought of) would have to be printed in three languages: Chinese, Korean, and sign language. The well-educated minority in Korea read Chinese and Korean; many more, educated only in the Occupation's adult education schools, read only Korean; and still more were completely illiterate.

For the latter, we devised a system of marks to distinguish one candidate from another. Outside and inside the voting booths there would be a picture of each contender with his name in Korean and Chinese and the sign or number of marks which would identify him on the ballot. The illiterate voter could thus put one and one together. But even such a simple procedure had to be explained and driven home. We printed thousands upon thousands of sample ballots in advance and distributed these widely throughout the remotest mountain areas.

Always hovering over us, of course, was the shadow of communist action, of not knowing in what ways the underground would attempt to sabotage the election, of having to be prepared for any eventuality.

It was soon obvious that the only possible way to bring off such a completely unprecedented election was to cover the country from tip to toe. Armed with unmistakable instructions from on top, we in Kangwon Province were able to commandeer two extra jeeps and a weapons carrier from Battalion to carry us and our equipment (films, projectors, generators, loud speakers, thousands of pounds of leaflets) into the hill country along the Parallel.

When the election was announced we had in Korea a few copies of an English-language film called *How We Elect Our Representatives*. This picture was aimed particularly at young Americans and described voting procedures quite unlike those to be used in Korea. It was obviously unsuitable, so a new picture called *The People Vote* was rushed into production in Seoul, and we received copies of it two weeks before registration day. To cap it all, the Army, which until then had scarcely noticed that an information program existed, now went all out with projectors, generators, tents, special rations, and extra gasoline.

Hong Shin was made commander in chief of our province-wide operation. Pak Chung Young was second in command. Each was given a mobile unit, complete with jeep, jeep driver, generator, screen and other projection equipment. Neither Hong nor Pak knew one end of a jeep or a generator from the other, and what they did to machinery was fantastic. I am not mechanically inclined myself, but I soon found it necessary to learn a few things: how to repair a generator in the pitch dark, how to set up a huge screen in a rice field so that thousands could see the film, how to patch a broken film, sometimes with nothing but scotch tape.

Both Hong and Pak were spellbinders when it came to soapbox oratory, and with no American except Elsie speaking the language of the country, we felt that the sacrifice of a few fenders and brake linings was a small price to pay for being understood. Most important of all was the fact that Hong and Pak had absolutely no illusions about communism. They had seen what the agrarian reformers were really doing, and had dedicated themselves to an all-out fight against the evil in the North. In the final analysis, it was often Elsie who was our *pièce de résistance*. When she got up to speak in her near-perfect Korean, a great hush always settled over the crowd. Sometimes I think that many of those mountain people who later exercised their franchise were really voting for Elsie.

We quickly developed a technique for approaching the people. Here again Elsie's experience was invaluable. Before my arrival in Korea she had spent nearly two years in the country. She had commanded a six-car special train, called the Silver Freedom Train, which had traveled almost every mile of the Korean railroad system. Under her direction were a group of enlisted men and a crew of Korean helpers. The train carried trucks, jeeps, and projection equipment so that the back country could be penetrated. Elsie had developed her own little spiel about democracy, using some posters she had devised. One set of posters dealt with communism in terms the farmers could understand. The poster on communism showed farmers pulling an oxcart with the ox riding in the cart. The poster on democracy, on the other hand, showed the farmers riding in the cart as was proper and the ox (representing government) doing his proper task of pulling.

The posters and the simple story they told were useful to us, and Elsie's knowledge of how to get the shows going also proved invaluable. The spots we selected were usually schoolyards, a parade ground, a wide street (if one could be found), or a rice field. During the hours in advance of our show we advertised the coming attraction in nearby villages. The crowds, humming with curiosity like a charged wire, had always settled into position, squatting on the ground, long before dark. Precurtain time was filled with recorded music by way of our public address system. Often I stepped up to the mike and spoke a few words in my halting and newly-learned Korean, much to the enjoyment of the crowd. Then came a long-winded introduction by an outstanding local celebrity, followed by an even longer and more impassioned speech by Hong Shin or Pak. When Hong's voice had given out, he retired, amid shouts of enthusiasm which thrilled him mightily, and we started the film.

It was unheard of for the picture to be run off without delays. Local electricity, where available, was never strong enough for the job. We always had to use our generator, hiding it behind a building or a haystack in order to muffle the sound. The long wire to the projector was a source of constant trouble. People tripped on it, and there were those who sometimes cut it. While the film was running, I patrolled the wire or hovered over the coughing generator. There was never a dull moment. It was a gruelling experience, stretching far into the night. In fact, we had to request the police to lift the usual curfews in order to finish our programs, particularly when we found that many of the audience had walked ten or fifteen miles to see the show.

I would not have believed that an audience could be held for four hours, even had the film been a dare-devil western (which ours certainly was not), but Hong Shin said that an evening so far outside the Korean farmer's normal routine was a tremendous event, and the longer the better. He turned out to be right. I was the one laid low.

Yet, instead of being able to sleep in a comfortable bed at the end of a harrowing day and strenuous evening, we would often have to maneuver the jeeps over the wildest mountain roads for hours before finding hotel accommodations. It was of course absolutely impossible to follow Army regulations which forbade Americans to use native hotels. We stopped where we found an inn, regardless of ownership. I also learned to like the forbidden Korean food and became quite accustomed to sleeping Korean fashion on the hard hot *ondal* floor.

Our teams continued to operate throughout the registration period, appearing nightly to as many as ten thousand. If an area proved slow to register, we sent a mobile unit for a return engagement or bombed it with thousands of leaflets dropped from planes. The plane drops were particularly effective and dramatic. We also gave particular attention to a few areas where communist elements proved troublesome. Pak Chung Young was beaten up once, we received a few threatening letters, and there were a few acts of minor sabotage. Otherwise we met relatively little obstruction.

Elsie and I tried to travel with the teams as much as possible, but my duties as advisor to the election commission kept me in Chunchon a good deal. We did make one long trip to the beautiful east coast of Korea, following the road where some of the bitterest fighting of the "police action" occurred two years later. As the crow flies, it is only some seventy-five miles from Chunchon to the Japan Sea. But as the jeep travels, it is one hundred and seventy-five miles of mountain after mountain and so many hairpin curves that one loses count. One hundred and seventy-five miles is an afternoon's drive in America. In Korea it is a major undertaking, completed—if all goes well—in one day. There were no filling stations along the way, so we had to carry with us extra gas, extra parts, and spare tires. On the east coast we stayed with Americans of a small Military Government detachment stationed at Kangnung. Along the way, we took our meals and spent the nights at the tiny Korean inns.

All the backbreaking work, all the sweat and trouble, was justified when the registration results came in. There had been a certain amount of betting among the Americans as to what the result would be, and my own guess of 70 per cent had been the highest made. What was my astonishment and delight to learn that in Kangwon Province, the province closest to the Parallel and therefore most easily infiltrated from the North, 96 per cent of the voting population had registered, the largest percentage in South Korea.

We could not slacken our pace for a moment, even though the registrations were in and had proved so encouraging. Now we had to see that those who registered also voted, and between times we inspected registration records and voting preparations to see that all would be in order and above criticism. We kept the mobile units constantly in the field. While I stayed in Chunchon, Elsie made a special investigation trip into the southernmost part of the province, to the city of Wonju and the coal fields of the Yongwol area. We began a radio program of our own over the tiny local station in Chunchon; we printed a steady stream of leaflets and instructions on voting; we made a countless number of speeches; we left no stone unturned to see that the first elections would be immune to communist attack and criticism.

The candidates began to come to us for advice. How were campaigns handled by candidates for office in the States? Could one attack his opponents? Wives asked whether or not it was permissible to help husbands get elected; whether it was democratic for a woman to vote for a man her husband opposed. We used the English discussion class we had organized in the early days of the center as a forum for a thorough discussion of the election. One of our members was a Mrs. Kim. We called her Mrs. Schoolteacher Kim to differentiate her from two other Mrs. Kims in the class. Mrs. Schoolteacher Kim was very much interested in the candidacy of a woman backed by the Chunchon Woman's Club. Her husband was on the other hand working for the Syngman Rhee candidate. Mrs. Kim was quite worried about the propriety of her actions but we assured her it was quite common in America for husband and wife to have differing political views. Mrs. Kim had a small baby, and she did her campaigning with the baby strapped, Korean style, on her back. Her candidate lost.

We became so intimately involved that I often wished I

could be one of the voters or could take a bigger part in the drama—an impossibility, of course, since it was incumbent upon Americans, as outsiders, to remain strictly neutral with regard to the contestants. There were three candidates running for the seat representing Chunchon city. One was a Syngman Rhee candidate, one was the women's candidate, and the third was an independent, a Korean businessman educated in America. Our own sympathies were with Teddy Pak, the independent. A serious problem arose when we discovered that Hong Shin was doing some special campaigning for Mr. Pak and was, moreover, using our equipment. We quickly put a stop to this, trying to explain that we, as election officials, had to be above reproach in everything that we did. It was a bit hard for Hong to understand but he accepted our ruling and we were restored to complete impartiality, at least outwardly!

On the day itself, almost every American civilian in Korea was pressed into service as an observer for the U. N. Commission. The commission members, numbering less than a dozen, could not expect to cover the hundreds of voting districts or even the two hundred electoral districts. We were divided into teams of two, an American and an interpreter, each team with an area to cover. Careful instructions were given us what to do in case of communist attacks. Every Korean police station was hooked into a telephone network which wound up in the office of the American police advisor in Chunchon. If trouble arose, we were to go to the nearest police station and call for help. We ourselves were not to interfere in any way. If we were asked for advice as election officials, we could give it, but our job was to observe and report.

Because of my experience (all four months of it!) I was assigned to the area directly along the Parallel between the Short and Long Russia crossings. Elsie was delegated as my interpreter. We were up before dawn that morning, along with other teams comprised of American residents of Seoul, since there were not enough American civilians in Kangwon Province to do the job. All that day we traveled, along the Short and Long Russia roads, down oxcart tracks never traversed by a jeep before, into remote mountain valleys, across creeks and rivers. By six o'clock there were long white queues outside the voting places. All available schools were used, and, for the overflow, private homes and shops.

In every province in Korea there were inspection teams like ours. As far as a very complete coverage of the day's activities indicated, there appear to have been few instances of pressure on the vote. Naturally, the forces of Dr. Syngman Rhee were well organized on election day, as they had a right to be. Their party workers were to be seen near every polling place. But party workers, of whatever candidate, held scrupulously to the required distance from the actual voting booths. The Korean police (there were those who claimed that the police, largely controlled by Rhee adherents, would dominate the voting) strictly minded their own business and only entered the booths to cast their ballots. During all that long weary day I did not see a single policeman nearer to the polling center than the three hundred yards required by law. The Korean election officials were meticulous and conscientious in seeing that the election laws were observed to the letter. I watched thousands of voters enter the booths; every voter that I saw cast his vote in absolute secrecy.

Surprisingly, there was not as much trouble as we had anticipated. One of our voting places was attacked by Communists soon after Elsie and I had completed our inspection. Here and there a few shots were fired. As soon as the polls were closed, election officials started moving the ballot boxes toward electoral district headquarters for counting. Because we had expected serious trouble en route, our troops were patrolling the main highways of the province. But since some of the voting places were as far as thirty miles from the nearest navigable track, the boxes were carried over the hills on the backs of coolies. In a few cases, boxes were captured and destroyed, but in general the election in Kangwon Province went off smoothly indeed. Again we topped all other provinces, with 92 per cent of the registered voters exercising their rights.

In only one province of Korea was there real obstruction. On the island of Cheju there was such terrorism that only a fraction of the people voted, and the election was ruled invalid until order could be restored. In some of the southern provinces there was election-day violence, a few murders, a few voting places attacked. Several candidates were killed. But in general the election was an enormous success. Our authorities did a magnificent job.

Nor did our duties end when the polls closed. General Hodge was determined that there be no opportunity whatsoever for criticism, and our work was not done until the last vote was counted. The election officials of our district were so anxious to complete the counting that they would not even wait until next morning to begin. As soon as the last boxes were in, at 10:00 P.M., they went to work, and Elsie and I took turns as official watchers throughout the night.

It was a long and painful procedure. There were practically no mechanical aids. Each long ballot was taken from the ballot box and inspected by watchers for the candidates; the vote was called out and the tally kept on an abacus. If there was any question about the validity of the ballot, if the X wasn't in quite the right place, it was brought to one of us for our opinion. "Our" man lost, but he lost honestly.

I have been shocked upon returning to America, to find that the Korean elections have been widely criticized here as undemocratic, as bought and rigged by the political forces of Syngman Rhee. Nothing could be further from the truth. There were undoubtedly cases of fraud and undue pressure; undoubtedly some votes were bought; undoubtedly some ignorant peasants voted a ticket they had been told to vote. But these cases were far too few to affect the returns. People voted for candidates favorable to Dr. Rhee because they wanted his men in office. As Americans, accustomed to the maximum of individual liberty, we may have pointed out to the Korean intellectual that Dr. Rhee had shown tendencies to be autocratic. The invariable answer was: "In this first phase of new political freedom we must have a good man who is strong and can hold the country in his hand. We must learn to creep on all fours before we can stand and walk."

The elections should have proved to us, without doubt in our minds, that the Korean people were and are capable of undertaking democratic governmental procedures. The election did a great deal for the nation. The emancipation of women was advanced years by the fact that women could vote their own choice. For the first time in half a century the average Korean felt that he had a stake in his own nation and its future. In spite of the efforts of the Communists, the people of South Korea went to the polls en masse, succeeding except on Cheju Island in casting a tremendous vote for a great number of candidates representing a great variety of political opinions. The general result was an undreamed of unification, a wave of patriotic fervor which should prove to us that when we make democracy a living thing, when we make it a personal crusade and work for it with our bare hands, truly respecting it ourselves, we can teach its rudiments with amazing speed. It is then contagious—if we follow it up with courage and encouragement.

The elections were in a measure an American victory, for the military and civilian elements in the Occupation worked well and intelligently together, and their weapons were effective. What Elsie and I did was not exceptional. Similar information teams, greatly augmented for the campaign, worked in every province. Perhaps the larger percentage of registrants and voters in our province was due in part to the fact that we spent more time in the field, working directly with election officials and the people. Both General Hodge and General Dean gave the Office of Civil Information much of the credit for the results. Several of us were called to Seoul to receive special commendations.

The real credit for the Korean elections goes to the Koreans. Without exception, the election officials with whom I worked were willing to forget personal politics and ambitions. The elections would have failed but for their painstaking organization work, their willingness to take advice, their ability to reach the people of all Korea.

Two years later I drove from the far south of Korea to Seoul on the second Korean election day. In this election Americans had no part; there was no great army of American advisors and observers fanned out over the land. Again the people responded, and again official pressure was kept to a minimum. I passed dozens of polling places that May 30, 1950, just a month before the communist invasion. Nowhere did I see police or party workers except where the law required them to be.

In this second election there were even more candidates than in the first, and many of them were opposed to the party in power. This alone should be an effective answer to those who criticize the Republic of Korea as a dictatorship. It is rare indeed when a dictator allows free elections and numberless opposition candidates to oppose him!

Chapter 4

Operation Cigarette

THERE was one act of communist retaliation that followed on the heels of the elections as night follows the day. The Russians, angered by the results of the voting, answered by cutting off all the electric power which came south from the great hydroelectric plants north of the Parallel, plants that have become familiar to many a weary soldier and marine during the dreadful retreat from the Chosin reservoir.

The Russians, of course, made it appear that their action had no relation to the election. The American Army had agreed that the Russian Occupation authorities would furnish electric power from North Korea in return for certain types of electrical equipment needed in the North. For months, freight cars loaded with insulators, light bulbs, generators, etc., had been standing in the Seoul railway yards. Some of the equipment had been accepted and shipped north (intelligence reported that it did not stop in North Korea, where it was intended to be used, but was shipped right on to Russia proper via the trans-Siberian rail line). The Russians suddenly announced that the Americans had refused to pay the agreed price and that the American electrical equipment offered did not meet specifications. Therefore, since the Americans had welshed, the Russians had no alternative but to cut the switches.

Our power situation had never been good, and the Russian action added considerably to the many inconveniences we faced in daily living. Far more important, without power South Korea's industries were crippled. General Hodge liked this no better than the Russians had liked the elections, and he decided to take positive action. He would not only do something to harass the North, but he would tell the true story to the North Koreans. He cast about for someone to put his ideas into effect and decided to make use of our Office of Civil Information. For that reason I was summoned to Seoul.

The plan was simple and repeated similar plans put in practice in other areas of the globe during the past ten years: the general's objective was to scatter anticommunist literature (newspapers, leaflets, etc.) throughout enemy controlled country. The communist regime in the North was, of course, under continual attack by South Korean radio stations, and our Office of Civil Information was already responsible for whatever propaganda work was being done; but it was not proving effective enough. Owners of radio sets were few, and listening could, in a measure, be controlled. Having been active along the China coast in 1943 and 1944, and having had experience in behind-the-lines activities, I was asked to plan and direct the new campaign. The whole operation was to be unofficial, which meant that I would be on my own. In other words, there would be unlimited confidential funds at my disposal, but if I got into trouble I would be disowned.

Returning to Chunchon, I discussed the whole project with Hong Shin. He rose to the idea like fish to bait, and his enthusiasm was infectious. He had all the answers, too. Actually, he had the best possible background for such an undertaking in the experience of his own Bible-smuggling days. Hong, good Christian that he was, had worked out quite a unique method of getting Bibles into North Korea long before he joined us. He even assured me that it would be the Christians north of the Parallel, who had received those Bibles in earlier days, that would now be our relay team of infiltration. Since they were Christian they could be counted on to be the most fanatically anticommunist of all Korean groups.

I gave Mr. Hong permission to start planning the program as soon as possible, impressing on him the necessity for the greatest secrecy. Not even our co-worker, Pak Chung Young, would be in the know. Hong needed little encouragement to make him careful on that score. He had received so many threatening messages as a result of his whole-hearted work in the elections, that he and his family were seriously frightened. A threat to kill him on election day had caused us to hide him in the back room—the inner sanctum of the shrine where the spirit of the Emperor was said to reside—for several days. It would be an understatement to say I felt sure he would be discreet.

He promised to bring me a contact who would be able to slip north and return. In spite of the fact that the border was increasingly well patrolled, there were hundreds of tiny trails and hidden passes in the mountains which could be exploited by the Koreans (the same mountain passes which were to be used time and again by the Chinese during the spring offensive of 1951). Refugees continued to come south. And, although it was much more difficult, passage north was still possible. Not for Americans, however. Except for a small liaison group in Pyongyang, no Americans had been north of the 38th in months.

Several nights later I stood alone, feeling somewhat adventurous and also mildly foolish, at the foot of a big pine on the upper slopes of Peacock Mountain. Two figures emerged from the shadows. I immediately recognized the quick, small figure of Hong, dark glasses and all, but when I was introduced to his companion I felt quite embarrassed. Could it be that Hong had misunderstood the nature of our project? Here was the most decrepit-looking, wizened hag I had ever seen. It was like meeting the Witch of Endor.

"What have we here?" I said to Hong, thoroughly nettled by what seemed an apparent farce.

"This woman will direct our movements above the Parallel," Hong said, completely undisturbed by my tone. "She may look old, and she is old—she thinks she is seventy-three—but she is honest, intelligent, and a Christian."

Obviously, there was nothing more to be said. The old woman was to be our agent, whether I liked it or not, and she turned out to be just what we needed. She was the brains of an organization of women peddlers who regularly went back and forth to sell scarce consumer goods in North Korea. In short, she and her companions were smugglers. Even the Communists wanted certain luxuries only to be obtained from the imperialist nations. American cigarettes were in the greatest demand in the North. Hong's find promised that if we could supply the cigarettes she would guarantee delivery into the hands of the North Koreans. From this meeting was born Operation Cigarette.

Though cigarettes were strictly rationed at our PX's, I had been promised whatever materials I needed and the money to pay for them. I sent a hurry call to Seoul, not for cartons of cigarettes but for whole cases. Shortly thereafter, we were under way with a brilliant plot, or at least one that lived on imagination.

We discovered that the covering of certain brands, those with no ripcord cellophane ribbon around the top, could be unfolded and closed again without indication of having been tampered with. We opened the packs, withdrew half the cigarettes, refilled the spaces with tightly rolled leaflets, and closed them again so perfectly that we hoped the most minute inspection would not disclose a fake package. The packing work had to be done late at night to insure secrecy. Since the rambling old geisha house in which we lived had Japanese paper walls and doors, it was doubly difficult to conceal our actions. We spoke, if at all, in whispers. The candlelight threw our shadows grotesquely on the walls. We crept to bed at dawn.

Our project brought with it new problems, and solutions

to old problems. There always seemed to be thousands of loose cigarettes in Elsie's room, and they had to be concealed, especially since she did not smoke. But since we now had an unlimited supply of cigarettes, all our ration cigarettes from the PX could be used to supplement the salaries of our employees.

We waited anxiously to hear how our first shipment of loaded cigarettes had fared. Even though a communist guard on the Short Russia road was bribed (yes, Communists can be bribed, too) to always allow the old women peddlers to pass, it did not guarantee that no search would ever be made. Men can be re-bribed.

Since the whole journey must needs be made on foot, we could not expect to see our carriers again for at least two weeks. We had instructed the old women to limit this trial run to the cities of Chorwon and Kumwha, close above the line. Indeed, it was two weeks to the day when Kimsie, the crone, appeared at Hong's house after midnight.

Her report was thrilling. Eleven women had crossed the Parallel and returned to tell of it! Twenty-two thousand anticommunist leaflets were fanning out somewhere in North Korea. Several of Mr. Hong's old friends and converts had sent word that they were eager to cooperate and would gladly act as forwarding and distribution agents at designated points. There seemed little doubt that the women were telling the truth. One contact in the North, willing to cooperate but suspicious, had sent his picture, with his "chop," or seal, on the back. Mr. Hong was to send his own picture and seal on the next trip so the man in the North would know without doubt the identity of the backers.

We never saw or knew the names of any of our women carriers, aside from Kimsie herself. She operated the whole liaison with the most extraordinary sense of what constitutes an underground, and with astonishing success up to a point. That point was the communist counterattack. Before it came we heard our operation denounced in no uncertain language over communist radio stations, and we guessed we were in for trouble.

Not having the vaguest idea of the routes we were using to push propaganda into their territory, or of the point or points of origin, the Communists suddenly posted a double-depth line of guards along the whole two-hundred-mile Parallel. Smuggling was all but stopped. The flood of refugees from the North dwindled to a trickle. Even so, Kimsie was determined to try the dangerous journey once more. To our sorrow, we let her go. It was her death warrant, and we felt we had signed it in spite of her insistence on going. We heard much later that she had been stopped and that a guard, looking for a smoke, had opened a package of cigarettes. Unfortunately, it was a doctored pack, and the leaflets spilled out at his feet. We didn't hear this from Kimsie herself. She never returned to tell it.

Then came the realization that we ourselves were under suspicion at the information center. Crudely written threats appeared on our desks, came slipped under our doors at night. Kimsie's son appeared, demanding payment from Mr. Hong for his mother's death. The son's interest came not from sorrow but from love of money, and his actions constituted a dangerous blackmail. Hong was badly frightened but still game. We paid off the son and were notified from Seoul that we could call it a day if we wished. We didn't. For the first time we had had a chance to do something concrete against the menace from the North, to deliver a small but effective blow against the Russian Bear. Clearly, Operation Cigarette as such would no longer be practical. But perhaps we could conjure up a new trick. Mr. Hong pulled one out of his hat and disappeared Seoul-ward for a week.

When he returned, he brought with him a well-dressed young Korean whom he introduced as "Mr. Pak, a businessman." Mr. Pak sat around and drank cokes with us all one afternoon, saying very little. To me he was the personification of an enigma. But that evening Mr. Hong explained him.

"Mr. Pak will be our new leader," he said. "He tells me that you will do."

I had been under the impression I did the hiring and firing around the place. Apparently not this time. I had been judged and found acceptable.

For our new act we selected a new stage, as it were: new routes, new personnel, new methods. This time men, not women, would cross into North Korea, and they would cross by way of the old Peking Pass above Seoul which was almost one hundred miles from our previous entrance near Short Russia. They would be under Pak's direction. Pak would never again come to Chunchon nor appear anywhere in our vicinity. He would meet Hong in Seoul for needed supplies. To make our coverage even better, we took another trip to the east coast and organized another group who would proceed north along the coast by foot and by boat to Wonsan. Two such attacks, almost two hundred miles apart, having no connection with each other and no visible tie-in with Chunchon, should certainly throw the Communists off the scent.

Instead of cigarettes we turned to drugs. People in stricken areas will always impoverish themselves further to obtain American medicines. I ordered ten thousand sulpha pills (to the amazement of headquarters in Seoul) and our boys went forth across the border disguised as modern medicine men. They carried envelopes of pills with the printed labels: "Pusan Medical Supply House." Since we had to put the formula on the envelopes, I carefully obtained directions from our Army doctor as to the uses and required dosages of our particular type of sulpha.

Although the technique was much more aboveboard than Operation Cigarette, it was no less effective. By a simple method, communist identification cards were obtained for each of our itinerant drug peddlers. We told a South Korean policeman on duty near the border that we needed a couple of dozen cards for souvenirs. This policeman was accustomed to searching refugees who came across the border, in order to determine whether they were carrying contraband or not. It was also his duty to forward their identification cards to Seoul. He was an ardent anti-Communist, and while he was examining refugees he gave them as much democratic propaganda as he could. He often came to ask us for materials to use in his "classes." Of course he realized that we wanted the identification cards for something more serious than their souvenir value and was glad to hand over a few to us. We made some slight changes on the cards, including change of photographs, and we were all set to go.

During the cigarette stage of our operation we had used material written and printed in Seoul. Now we began to produce our own leaflets. Among Mr. Hong's many church interests was an orphanage on whose board of directors he served. The orphanage operated a small printing plant and did job work to help cover expenses. Soon the orphans were busily engaged in printing our pill envelopes and the special leaflets I wrote.

In a few weeks the "Pusan Medical Supply Comany" was running so smoothly that we were able to smuggle almost anything across the border with very little danger. South Korean newspapers by the hundreds went north; leaflets and even battery radio sets were carried to reliable friends. We printed special lists of South Korean radio programs, tempting North Koreans to tune in to the programs that might lower morale in the North by bringing in a little more truth from the outside world. The operation, naturally, worked two ways. Our men brought back a great deal of valuable information from the northern provinces: reports of the economic situation, Party squabbles, the failure of land reform, the treatment of workers, the presence of Chinese and Russians in the North Korean military, etc.

We were amateurs and, more than likely, professional undercover agents will laugh at our tiny projects. Operation Cigarette operated on a shoestring. It was an unofficial project, not even mentioned in the record books; and it was carried on only because a few top Army men in Korea were willing to let us try to answer some of the enemy's tactics in kind. If the medical infiltration had been continued through 1949 and 1950, we might well have learned of the huge rearmament and training program north of the Parallel, and of the attack being prepared against South Korea. Unfortunately, the project was abandoned after General Hodge relinquished his command to the diplomats of the Department of State.

Even though we finally succeeded in pushing as many as two hundred thousand leaflets a month into the North, even though our distributors were at work in the highest echelons of the communist government, the good we accomplished was only a beginning.

I am convinced, nevertheless, by the effectiveness of these slight and inexpensive campaigns of truth, that if the millions living inside communist Asia could be reached by personal contact in ways such as ours, wonders might be forthcoming. The dissident elements, the wavering and undecided, the fiercely rebellious—all these might somehow be reached and welded together if given concrete, intimate knowledge of outside support. I have experienced the terror it is to find a leaflet or threatening letter on one's desk. One begins to suspect his own employees, every visitor who comes to call. There is nothing so frightening as the unknown.

The long coast of China, so easily penetrated from Formosa or Hong Kong, offers great opportunity for similar penetration. The method works. It reaches individual men and women far more effectively and far less expensively than do the radio broadcasts from New York. A propaganda war today cannot be won from offices in Washington or from 250 West 57th Street, New York, where the Voice of America broadcasts in twenty-five languages a day. It cannot be won by merely continuing to tell our allies that they are our friends. What of those who live behind the communist curtains, in hope or in apathy, those who live in the many areas where poverty is great and radios are few? The propaganda war must be carried to the field. We must speak to those we have lost, in terms they understand. We must make our contact more immediate. We must speak to the artisan and the farmer, the coolie and the businessman. We must speak through the written word, whether it is smuggled in or dropped from balloons. Above all, we must speak person to person, through man to man contact.

Operation Cigarette lasted only a few months, but it had penetrated the skin, if not the iron curtain, of the Communists to the north. At least we could not help feeling that the attack, made upon us at the 38th Parallel not long after the operation folded, was a direct result of my part in the intrigue. We had gone picnicking and sightseeing to the 38th one afternoon, with friends from Washington. It was considered a sporting adventure to drive to the Parallel and try to catch a glimpse of the blond Russian giants who guarded the opposite side. There was a period when the roads north from Seoul were clogged with Americans on Sunday afternoons, all bound for the border.

This afternoon we had driven up a steep narrow road to where it dead-ended smack against the border at a bridge across the north branch of the Han River. My passengers, including Elsie, had just stepped from the car, and I was still at the wheel, when we were suddenly machine-gunned from ambush. While the others dropped down into a rugged ditch below the road and started crawling to safety, I backed the car, already riddled with bullets, to a turning point, picked them up, and fled to safety. No one was wounded. If this was vengeance it had not succeeded. I had a twinge of satisfaction that perhaps Operation Cigarette had drawn their fire.

Chapter 5

The Thirty-eighth Parallel

OPERATION CIGARETTE did not, of course, take our full time. In fact, much of the important part of the cigarette work we did at night, in the off hours. Meanwhile, the normal work of an American information center continued: distributing our weekly Korean language publication *World News;* taking trips with the motion-picture unit; putting on special programs at the information center. In order to reach as many people as possible, to bring them up the long flight of steps to the shrine, we carried on a great variety of activities. We had athletic games in the great courtyard to attract the youngsters. We set up replicas of an American county fair with industrial and agricultural exhibits. We held English oratorical contests.

In addition to these or similar activities, developed in all our information centers, I branched into the field of music in a large way. A fine symphony orchestra had been organized in Seoul under the direction of a talented American musician, Rolf Jacoby. It occurred to me to bring the orchestra to Chunchon for a concert in the courtyard of the shrine. It proved to be quite an undertaking, since the normal transportation facilities provided by the "doodlebug" were not enough to bring a hundred-piece orchestra and its equipment to Chunchon. A special train with its own locomotive was commandeered. A group of Chunchon women undertook to feed the musicians. Battalion loaned us trucks to bring them from the railroad station to the foot of Peacock Mountain where the coolies took over to carry the heavy instruments up the steps.

The day of the concert dawned sparkling and clear, with the intense blue sky for which the Korean mountain country is famous. I had no idea how well the Parallel folk would respond to classical music or whether they would even come. But come they did, by the thousands. The afternoon concert played to ten thousand people who overflowed the great courtyard into the pines almost to the top of Peacock Mountain. It was a scene never to be forgotten: the orchestra playing in the great hall with the red-lacquered doors wide open; the backdrop of brilliantly tiled roof and green pine trees; the adults dressed in white, but the children in the pinks, reds, and purples reserved for holidays. The crowd that assembled in the evening was almost as large, and certainly as rapt. Whether they understood the music or not, whether they had ever heard the names of the composers, these mountain folk listened with an appreciation that would do justice to an audience in Carnegie Hall.

Nor was our work limited to the shrine or even to Chunchon. The United States Air Force provided us with one of the most memorable opportunities of these months. Our B-29's, based on Okinawa, were making a practice flight far out into the Sea of Japan between Japan and southern Siberia. Maybe visibility was bad, perhaps the maps were incorrect. Anyway, they mistakenly bombed a handful of rocks and small islands far off the Korean coast but belonging to Korea. Twelve Korean fishing vessels were sunk and numerous fishermen killed, wounded, or drowned. There was an immediate uproar, especially over the communist radio. It was reported that the planes were manned by Japanese pilots in training, that we had purposely ordered the attack. The South Korean press was rather upset about the mistake, and in general it was an uncomfortable situation.

The main island of the group, Ulong-do ("do" meaning island), lay one hundred and twenty miles off the coast of

PEACOCK MOUNTAIN

VISITORS AT THE SHRINE

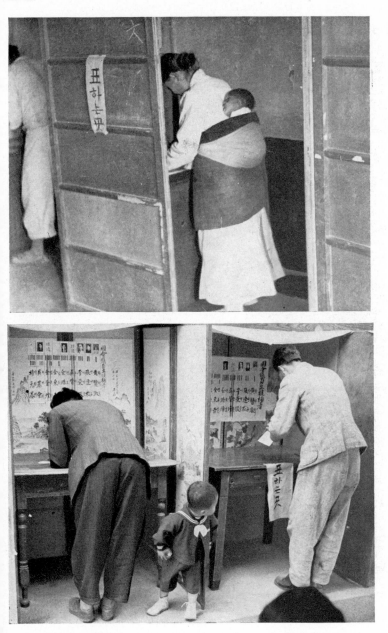

Above: WOMAN VOTING. *Below:* ELECTION DAY, 1948

THE PEOPLE VOTE, MEN IN ONE LINE AND WOMEN IN ANOTHER

southern Kangwon Province. It was more or less in my territory, so I asked Seoul for permission to go to Ulong-do, make
an official apology and do some remedial propaganda work.
With permission granted, Elsie, Hong Shin, Pak Chung
Young, and two or three assistants headed for the east coast
with me. We drove over the wild mountains along the head-
waters of the Han River, and dropped five thousand feet to
the Japan Sea through the lovely Kangnung Pass. Then we
drove another forty miles along the coast to the port of
Mukho.

We had no written instructions, no authoritative orders,
which meant we were obliged to make our own arrangements
for transportation. With the help of an American port engineer we located a fifty-foot harbor tug which, we were assured, was seaworthy and could make the trip. She was named
the *Ee-Che-Sung*, which meant, according to Mr. Hong,
"Second Son's Castle." The captain said he had made the trip
before and was ready and willing provided I could supply the
needed diesel oil. By going to a company of American troops
stationed near Kangnung and exaggerating the importance
of my mission, I got the oil. With oil, generator, motion-picture equipment, and our Korean helpers stowed aboard, we
took to the open sea.

Almost immediately a storm broke, everyone turned green,
and we were blanketed by fog. I was about to give the captain
orders to turn about when the fog lifted and we kept on, and
on, and on—for twelve hours without sighting land. Then far
off to the south of us, I saw the dim outlines of Ulong Island
and its 3,200-foot central peak. We had missed it and were
already deep in North Korean waters. By the time we had
turned and approached the island, it was dark, and the captain
chose this moment to admit he had never been there before,
and had no idea where the one and only harbor was located!
We spent until midnight edging around the island. For the
most part, the shore line went straight up and down in five-
hundred-foot cliffs. At last we spotted what looked like a

harbor entrance, and at two in the morning we dropped anchor and went ashore. By luck, we were off Ulong City.

Our subsequent three days on and around the island provided us with an experience unsurpassed in strangeness and
discovery. We were the second party of Americans to visit
Ulong-do in ten years, and Elsie was the first white woman
many of the islanders had ever seen. We gave a movie on the
school grounds which attracted, we estimated, seven thousand people in a city of five thousand. It was a smash hit.
After we had run through our meager stock of "current"
films, the people wanted more. So, even though the elections
were two months past, we dug out *The People Vote* and its
appeal was still box-office.

We visited the survivors of the bombing in a local hospital.
We were wined and dined by the city officials, who begged
that we remain and give a show at the other end of the island.
In spite of the unfortunate bombing, we were received with
open arms. America and Americans came first on Ulong-do.
I was greatly pleased with the reception and the general
friendliness, but it took Mr. Hong to explain the reason behind it all. Quite frankly, said he, Americans were popular
because there had been no Americans there in the past.

Be that as it may, we cruised the shores of the island, with
its magnificent cliffs and rock formations, and gave a second
performance. The location was such that we could not land
our heavy generator, and we were forced to improvise. We
kept the generator on the tug, anchored the boat off shore,
and strung a line to the rocky beach. We set up the screen on
a stranded fishing junk, the projector on another. The crowd
sat on the rocks, on other boats, and among the pines on the
hillside across the bay. But still another emergency arose.
Halfway through a picture, the wire from tug to shore
parted company. To fill the gap, Elsie mounted a junk and
gave an impromptu address on democracy. All in all we had
won the day for the U. S. Air Force with a naval maneuver!

While the concerts, the contests of every description, the

special shows, and the trip to Ulong Island undoubtedly high-
lighted our official reports of that spring and summer, it was
a period of great importance to me for another reason. Operation Cigarette had developed in me a burning interest in
North Korea. The Parallel, and what lay behind it, began
more and more to fascinate me.

It was but a thirty-minute drive to the roadblock at Short
Russia and an hour up the longer road that followed the Soyang River to the Long Russia crossing. There was always
ample excuse for going toward the Parallel on business. For
instance, these trips provided us with the very best method
of distributing our weekly *World News*. Published in simple language, this one-sheet weekly newspaper covered activities of the American Army in Korea, world news of interest to the people, and special articles about Korea. For thousands of Koreans, it was the only newspaper available.

Elsie first suggested that we take bundles of papers with us
when we left the center and scatter them along the way. To
me it seemed a bit undignified to drive down the streets of
Chunchon, or along the highways, tossing out newspapers.
But once the ice was broken, I began to enjoy it. Bundles of
papers became a part of every expedition, long or short. I
found that I could make a farmer lay down his tools, distract
the bustle in a village market, even bring a long Korean fu-
neral procession to a full halt, with a mere handful of papers.
There would be an immediate scramble for possession. A part
of the interest was of course that of getting something free,
but often we would pass back along the same routes and see
the white-clad farmers earnestly studying the stories or talking over the news in animated discussion.

During the hot weather months I made use of the Han
River swimming holes as a pretext for getting as close to the
Parallel as possible. Both the north branch of the Han and
the Soyang River ran clear and cool, and there were some
lovely deep pools in both streams. The Army had made swimming illegal, punishable by summary court-martial. An Army

medical "expert" had reported that the disease schistosomiasis was endemic to Korea. The Army had never bothered to ask the missionary doctors whether this were true (it was not) but had automatically made swimming in fresh water "off limits." However, we were so far from Seoul, and the water so inviting, that such a regulation was scarcely enforceable.

Thus, gradually, we were seeing more and more northerners at first hand. I was often the first to meet a refugee as he emerged from the mountain passes onto the South Korean highways. I also often passed the gates of the huge refugee camp in the Soyang River valley, one of three maintained by the Army to collect, interrogate, and DDT the increasing horde.

One hot Sunday afternoon we passed a police station where a little knot of refugees was awaiting truck transportation down the valley to the camp. There was one strikingly beautiful girl, obviously ill and in great pain, being carried by an exhausted man. We stopped and picked them up in our jeep and took them to the camp.

As we drove down the twisting road, Elsie spoke to them, asking about their lives, their trip south, why they had left their homes in the North. They were a brother and sister, and they had travelled a hundred miles walking by night, the brother carrying the girl on his back. They were hungry and frightened, without relatives in the South, half believing the communist stories of the brutal South Koreans and Americans. At first they were almost speechless. We were probably the first white people they had ever spoken to, but slowly we got their story.

Theirs had been a farming family in the North, but the father was too old to work for the Communists, and the son was too stubborn. Land reform had passed them by because they refused to join in Party activities. Then the girl injured her foot and it became infected. When she sought medical attention she was turned away. After all, they were not Party members, and the family had been "uncooperative." The good things in life were reserved for those who saw the light. After gangrene had set in, the brother made the decision to make the trek south, in the hope that in the American zone he could find a doctor who would treat his sister.

It was hard to get the full story. There were gaps in it that roused our curiosity, but too soon we were outside the gates of the camp. We saw to it that the girl got immediate medical attention and left the two almost speechless with thanks for the little thing we had done. As we drove away I saw the two cards lying on the ground, identity cards issued by the Peoples' Republic to all its citizens. The brother had undoubtedly "lost" the cards, perhaps fearing that even possession of such things might brand him as a Communist.

During the following months, we began to make a special effort to interview refugees, sometimes at the camp, sometimes at the shrine, sometimes along the Han River road. For me it was a novel and eye-opening experience. I had just come from two years in the Department of State: one year as director of the U. S. Information Service in China under the Marshall Mission; and another year in Washington. Nine out of ten of my colleagues in China and Washington were either so anti-Chiang or so pro-communist that I had heard little but praise of Far Eastern communism. For almost three years I had moved and worked in an environment where one was outcast if he did not violently attack the status quo in Asia and talk approvingly of the books and articles extolling the new reform movements there. I had myself expressed some criticism of the Chiang regime, not in an effort to win support for the Communists, but because I thought that some criticism might help bring reforms. I had no leanings whatsoever toward communism, but I had begun to wonder what it was all about.

Now along the Short Russia and Long Russia roads I was beginning to hear at first hand just what this great "reform" movement meant, or did not mean, to those who had lived under it. Also I was beginning to have, for the first time, a clear picture of what all this might mean to me as an American. I have never studied Marx or Lenin, and I know little about the theory of Communism even now. But I did get from the lips of refugees an idea of some of the aims of communism as these aims might affect me and my children.

I heard over and over again the story of what communism teaches about America. I talked to people who were actually frightened when they saw me, an American. I learned that we are described as a brutal, corrupt people, a people having no right to a place of power in the world. I learned that in order to have what the Communists call world peace, America as a power must be destroyed. I learned how the good things we do are distorted and turned against us, and how the failures of our democracy are used, told over and over again, added to, and embroidered upon, to convey a picture of us as a truly despicable, cruel, and imperialistic nation. I heard from the lips of scores of Christians what had happened to their churches and their pastors. I learned that the Communists tell their people that Christianity is nothing but an agency of American imperialism and must be stamped out in its present form. I heard of whole congregations either liquidated or driven underground or into exile.

On one occasion I picked up what, in my opinion, was a very reliable report that Chinese communist officers had actually been seen along the Parallel, inspecting North Korean positions. The report went to the State Department. I learned also, from North Korean refugees and South Koreans alike, and *two years before the invasion*, that the Chinese Communists would enter any conflict between North and South Korea. South Koreans thought it probable that they could eventually check a purely North Korean attack; but if the North Koreans had Chinese help, and the Russian help that the realistic Korean took for granted, they would be helpless. Yet there are supposedly intelligent people in America who can see no world pattern in communism, who can see no relationship between what has happened in Korea and what can and probably will happen in Indochina. And what about Burma, Malaya, and India, to name a few more danger areas?

Unofficially, the Department of State has tried with considerable success to convince Americans that the Chinese entered the Korean war because they were menaced, that there is relatively little Russian planning behind what has happened in Korea. The realistic South Korean knows better. The full extent of Russian participation, of Russian arrogance, of our own naïveté has never been known.

While the Russians were patrolling the Parallel, they often created incidents as flagrant as those in Germany. Americans were sometimes picked up at bayonet point as far as half a mile south of the border. And long after the US-USSR Joint Commission negotiations had collapsed, the Russian liaison mission stayed on in Seoul, acting as if it owned the place. On many occasions I have seen the Russians enter our PX to stock up on every kind of American supply. Their special trains moved in and out of the Seoul railroad yards. Once, Elsie went to the yards to visit the Silver Train which was parked there. After talking to old Korean friends she stepped down from our train, only to be met by the guns of two Russian guards. Bolts clicked, and for a moment it looked like trouble. Yet this happened in a railroad yard controlled by the American Army, within a few steps of an American train, and months after the US-USSR Joint Commission, the last pretext for Russians to be in Seoul, had folded.

It is true that the Russians eventually withdrew from the Parallel. But our friends from the North, our refugee contacts, continued to bring us news of the huge Russian military mission in Pyongyang, of the Russian experts that swarmed over the land. The Russians merely played a game of musical chairs. The general who had formerly commanded Russian troops in North Korea became the new Russian ambassador to the North Korean People's Republic. As such he was still the boss, with a capital "B." Yet how many Americans have swallowed the line that the events in Korea were but a matter of argument between North and South, that events developed without Russian master-minding and were in fact brought on by the belligerence of the South Koreans instead of by the cold war already raging throughout the entire world between communist Russia and the West.

One of the oft-repeated lines of communist propaganda in North Korea was that the Americans were arming Japan, were using Japanese troops in Korea, and were eventually going to give Korea back to the Japanese. This approach had considerable effect, playing as it did on Korean hatred of the Japanese. And I often wonder what impression the refugees at the Chunchon camp received when, after they had been DDT'd and checked by a doctor, they were led into a big tent to be interrogated by our intelligence staff. For the Army used Nisei Japanese soldiers, who spoke no Korean and were forced to interrogate the refugees in the Japanese language so utterly loathed by the Koreans.

I could tell a hundred typical stories of what it is like to live in a people's republic. The pre-dawn security checks; the announcement to a shop owner or innkeeper that, as of the next day, he no longer owned his place of business because he had not properly cooperated with the Party.

I remember the story told us by a man named Pang who had voted in one of the "democratic" elections held in the North. Pang was a resident of Haiju, a large city immediately north of the Parallel. The Russian-sponsored North Korean Government wished to determine whether it would be safe to hold a free election. One hundred citizens were asked to participate in a sort of Gallup Poll. The participants were assured the vote would be secret, that no one would be punished for his vote. The result was a shocking write in for, of all persons, Syngman Rhee, that "dictator," that "agent" of American imperialism! Sixty-one per cent of the people polled in Haiju expressed their preference for Rhee. The regime naturally decided that a free election was dangerous, and a typical communist election was held in August 1948.

We still have a copy of a report, in diagram form, on just how free the election was. The white and black box system was used. Those who voted "yes" for a single slate of candidates placed their ballots in the white box; those who voted "no" used the black box. There was a "secret" voting booth in each polling place. At the entrance to the booth were four desks. Behind one sat the official who gave out the blank ballot, furtively noting the number of the voter on the back. Next was the number checker. Then a party watcher and, finally, an "unofficial" observer. But as if all these precautions were not sufficient, inside the booth, standing over the boxes, were two women watchers; and, outside, thirty policemen were on guard.

We also still have the original copy of another report on free elections, communist style. This report was given to us by three refugees at the camp: a thirty-six-year-old carpenter, a former employee of the communist post office, and a once prosperous contractor who had been working as a day laborer since the Russians occupied North Korea. Election day in August 1948 found these men and their families in Hwachon. The following is their collective story of activities prior to and during election day.

Publicity started a few weeks before election. We were told that only an election could reunite North and South Korea. Fifteen days before election we registered. Even though we were not residents of Hwachun, we and our wives registered. Two days before election some officials came around and explained the election to us. Some were threatened. We were told that the wells of people who did not vote would be poisoned. Voting started at 5:00 A.M. We arrived at the voting place at ten o'clock and there were 160 people in line. We first showed registration slips to the voting officials. The number of the registration slip was placed on our ballot so that it would be possible to know how we voted. As we went into the voting place all the officials pointed out the white box and urged us to place our ballot in that box. We were instructed to receive the ballot in both hands. The ballot was small and could be concealed. The two boxes were supposedly close enough together so that by stretching out our arms we could reach either box and in that way could slip the marked ballot into one box or the other without being detected. But it didn't work that way because the ballot boxes were so far apart that it was obvious which box the ballot was placed in. The only secrecy was a waist-high screen. Voting stopped at one o'clock and the results were announced the next morning at nine. Two people stood right over the ballot boxes, supposedly to help the old and ignorant country people. We all voted because we were afraid not to and we were on our way south to freedom. Others in the village did not vote. They were taken away at gun point. The next day the election officials announced a 100 per cent vote.

In particular, I got an entirely new conception of what land reform actually meant to the people, a conception since fortified by firsthand accounts from my home province of Fukien in China where the people have been completely disillusioned by the vaunted land reform program of the Chinese Communists. The peasants around my old home town of Futsing are poorer, pay heavier taxes, and go hungrier than ever before. There is a new, wry saying among them: "Bring back that corrupt bandit Chiang!"

Since the American Military Government was at this time inaugurating a system of land reform among the South Koreans, it was important for us to know and understand the intentions of the Communists in this respect. The dangers inherent in misapplied land reform are enormous. The Military Government, together with South Korean officials, formulated a land reform program which has since been carried on by the Republic of Korea in spite of the war and which has reduced farm tenancy in South Korea by 70 per cent. The program began in the summer of 1948 with the sale of 700,000 acres of the best farm land in South Korea, all formerly owned by Japanese companies and individuals.

While I was selling the idea of land reform to the Korean people of Kangwon Province, I was learning about the land reform in the North. I have since learned that my information was accurate. The ECA officials who were sent into North Korea during MacArthur's push to the Yalu River were able to make an on-the-spot study, and their story was released to the American press months ago, though the press has scarcely passed it on to the American people.

They found that in March 1946 the Communists carried out a wide distribution of land in a period of twenty-five days, for the purpose of gaining public favor. But in 1948 they took it all back in order to make a redistribution, giving choice grants to Communist Party favorites. Many of the farmers receiving land had no actual title to it. They had what the Communists called "utilization rights." This enabled the People's Republic to throw a farmer off the land by withdrawing the rights, thus reducing him to slave status. In 1947 a production tax in kind of 27 per cent of his rice crop and a 25 per cent tax on all his other crops was levied. Furthermore, irrigation fees, army levies, and various other special taxes raised his taxes out of all proportion.

My talks with refugees supported what I was able to learn elsewhere about communist reforms. In fairness it should be admitted that some of the reforms were genuine at first. They were often used as bait to obtain public support while the police state had time to develop its complete control. In the final analysis, reform became a myth, a myth still believed by a surprising number of intellectuals in America.

What was the story of land reform in South Korea? Beginning in 1945, as soon as the American Occupation authorities got under way, the rent of all farm land was reduced to one-third of the principal crop. In 1948 began a sale in which we had a part: nearly 700,000 acres of land were sold to 500,000 farmers. (Remember that an average South Korean farm household tills about 2.5 acres.) This sale reduced tenancy from 70 per cent to 40 per cent.

In June 1949 the Republic of Korea passed legislation to enable one million tenant farmers to purchase 1,800,000 acres of tillable land. Payments were set at 30 per cent of the principal crop for five years. Land owners were reimbursed in national bonds to the value of the crop payment, and these bonds could and can be used to buy factories and other industries formerly owned by the Japanese. The program was in effect a double-barreled one, reducing farm tenancy on the one hand, and creating a new industrial business class on the other. To date, in spite of the war, 1,029,000 acres of land have been redistributed.

To the average person in America, where thousands upon thousands own acreage in the hundreds, the land problem in Korea will seem strange. In all South Korea, for instance, there were 295,816 landowning families. Of these, 213,453 owned less than 2.5 acres, while an additional 81,563 owned up to 100 acres. Only eight hundred families owned more than 100 acres. The problem was that many owned no land at all but through the years had rented from the owners. The object of land reform was, therefore, to see that there were more owners, that available land was more equitably distributed, and that large holdings, where they occurred, should be divided among the tenants.

Land reform, even the selling of those 700,000 acres of Japanese land in 1948, was not accomplished without opposition. The few who did own large acreage did not at all take to land reform. There were influential men who fought it step by step. Some of these were members of the national assembly, perhaps even members of the cabinet. But, for those who might criticize this opposition, I would like to ask what would happen in America if, for example, we attempted to force people to sell all the land they held in excess of five hundred acres? I can imagine the anguished cries, the lobby that would soon be at work in Washington, the senators and representatives who would be shouting from the housetops. Any reform that steps on toes—and all reforms do—creates a powerful and vocal opposition. The Korean landowner was no exception, and the Korean politician responded exactly as an American politician would respond.

I could not help feeling that I had a vested interest in the Republic of Korea. I had been, in a way, a midwife at its birth. I saw many things in the years 1948 to 1950 that I did not like. I saw corruption. I saw a great deal of inexperience that led to a myriad of mistakes. But I always remembered the stories from the North and realized that at its worst, the new government of South Korea was a hundred times better than that of the People's Republic. The South Korean Government may not have enough respect for the rights of human beings, but the Communists do not even admit that human beings exist. In other words, my education on the Parallel that summer made me realize as never before that our position with respect to Chiang was a deliberate phony, and that we are now running into the same danger as regards Syngman Rhee.

What Americans often fail to realize when they speak against President Rhee is that he was honestly elected by the majority opinion, if not the vote (since he was actually elected to the presidency by deputy). They do not realize, when they attack Chiang Kai-shek and the Nationalist Government of China, that in Asia democratic governments must start from scratch. Any such government must of necessity be placed in the hands of inexperienced, sometimes very young men. I have already described the manner in which the Japanese shut Koreans out of positions of responsibility. Koreans were not permitted to become school principals, much less cabinet ministers. Though Dr. Rhee is a scholar and a gentleman, truly educated, he has had no government experience, except by observation.

Under these circumstances it was only natural that the fledgling republic should make mistakes. It would be a miracle if it had not. And one could hardly expect it to be an American model of the democratic system overnight. Indeed, why should we have been so surprised that the Korean constitution, drafted immediately after the elections by the two hundred elected national assemblymen, did not follow ours very closely? Great powers were placed in the hands of the chief of state. The constitution was also socialistic in nature, whether by choice of the assemblymen or by advice of American experts I do not know. The railways, the utilities, were nationalized. Since every large industry had been Japanese owned (all Japanese property was known as Vested Property), it too was nationalized. To my mind herein lay one great mistake. Although the men who were elected to political offices rarely were trained businessmen, yet the constitution placed economic as well as political development completely in their hands.

The steps taken by the new national assembly were taken one at a time but with an unusual display of popular consent at first. When Syngman Rhee, who had been elected for a four-year term by an almost unanimous vote of the national assembly, was inaugurated on August 15, 1948, there were wildly enthusiastic celebrations all over Korea. General MacArthur flew from Japan for the occasion. In Chunchon, fifty thousand people turned out to hear speeches and cheer the first president.

Dr. Rhee immediately stepped into a situation no American president has yet faced. He had a powerful and determined enemy within his gates. Here in America our battle with communism is a legal battle, carried from court to court, with meticulous concern for the rights of the Communists. Here, police are not murdered by Communists, nor are vast acts of sabotage committed. In Korea, there were thousands of undercover agents. Within a few months of Dr. Rhee's inauguration, bloody rebellion broke out in units of the South Korean Army. Guerilla bands on Cheju Island, supplied by sea from China and North Korea, held the residents in terror for months. I flew over the island, which constitutes one of South Korea's provinces and shall never forget the sight of villages burning from one horizon to the other.

Full of confidence, inspired by the popular grant of the power to act quickly, Rhee and his associates moved (perhaps too quickly and harshly at times) to mop up the dissident factions. The Korean national police too often continued to be brutal and were not always careful to prove guilt. The roughshod methods of the police created a vicious circle: a case of brutality against a Communist or supposed Communist provoked retaliation from communist "awakened" villagers. This in turn provoked the police to further excesses. But let us not forget that we supervised and trained the police during three years of occupation.

Further to complicate and weaken a far from stable situation, the Department of State took over from the Army of Occupation at a most inopportune moment. It came upon the scene, moreover, filled with some of the same naïve notions that had already lost us China.

Chapter 6

AMIK

THE American Occupation of Korea ended officially on August 15, 1948. That summer was a season of farewell parties; American officers and men began the withdrawal while new civilian faces, fresh from Washington and full of new ideas, took their places. Operation Cigarette ended for want of interest. Rumors were the order of the day for Americans; rumors, and vacation trips to Shanghai, now being menaced from the north. Hundreds of Occupation personnel, knowing their days in the Orient were numbered, took the special vacation trips offered by Northwest Airlines, reaching Shanghai in four hours, there to savor the luxuries of hot baths and good food.

I took the trip myself and laid over a couple of planes so that I could spend two weeks with old friends, Chinese and American. It was a discouraging trip for me. I was full of Korea, the triumph of the elections, the communist threat. But I found not one sympathetic ear, not one person who wasn't anxious to argue, to repeat the vicious stories of Syngman Rhee's "steal" of the election, of brutality and corruption in the newest republic on earth. I spent one evening at the home of John William Powell, the son of J. B. Powell, former crusading editor and foreign correspondent in Shanghai. It was as if we were gathered around the deathbed of a wealthy and once beloved relative, whose will might mean much to all of us. But, instead of hushed respect, all present sought to tell the ugliest possible story about the dying. It is interesting now to see that of those who met in Bill

Powell's home that night, five have gone over to the Communists in China, including Powell himself. These young Americans are now adding their voices and influence to the fight against America and against their own land, Powell as editor of the *China Review*. One other who was there that night has since spent many an hour before a congressional committee, defending his own loyalty and that of the organization he represents.

I had returned to China with more than a vacation in mind, more than the pleasant renewal of friendships. I returned with an intense curiosity to see what changes in official attitude had taken place in our Asian policy. As an officer of the OWI in China from 1943 to 1945, and later when I was in the China service of the Department of State, I had been a more or less puzzled observer of the Administration's evaluation of the aims and strength of the Chinese Communists. During that time, the Department of State was eagerly promoting two objectives in the Far East. One was to persuade its personnel in China and elsewhere that Chinese communism was what China needed; that if we were patient we would find that we could work shoulder to shoulder with the Communists; that if Chiang was not deposed, at least he should bring the Communists into a coalition government. The other, though not official nor so well organized, was none the less vicious. It was designed to discredit General MacArthur and to picture him as a power-driven reactionary who would ruin our hopes for developing a true democracy in Japan.

I was young and new to government in those days. I know well what impact the special briefings, lectures, staff meetings, and policy conferences, in which these issues were constantly discussed, had upon me. I was duly impressed. We were also made to see, clearly enough, what side our promotion was buttered on. Two factions formed within the State Department, but advancement usually hinged upon belonging to the anti-MacArthur and pro-Chinese-Communist school. The debates, for and against, became extremely bitter. MacArthur was attacked in language unbecoming to diplomats, with fierce personal animosity. On the other hand, the anti-Communists did not help the cause by ascribing virtues to Chiang Kai-shek that he and his government quite obviously did not possess. Objectivity flew the coop of the State Department.

In returning to China, I was also returning to scenes of a rather personal disaster. In 1946 and 1947, I was director of the United States Information Service in China. One day in late '46 I received a cable from Washington directing me to prepare a report on the propaganda activity of the Russians and the Chinese Communists in China. The report was for the Department of State but had been specifically requested by a congressman, a member of the House Foreign Affairs Committee who was especially interested in the Far East. I went to work. I listened to Russian radio programs, visited Russian information centers, saw Russian films, and read the Russian subsidized newspapers, the Chinese communist newspapers.

My report covered sixty-four pages, and no one who read it could fail to realize how viciously anti-American the communist line in China had become. (It has remained the same to this day.) Nor could anyone fail to see that the lines of the Russians and the Chinese Communists ran parallel; merged, in fact, as one slanderous tirade. American soldiers then, as now, were accused of brutalities with all the trimmings; American pilots were said to be piloting Nationalist planes and bombing defenseless civilians; the U. S. Marines (then garrisoned in Tientsin) were accused of rape, pillage, and using Chinese farmers for target practice. UNRRA, then active in China, was called a tool of American imperialism, exactly as ECA, Mutual Security, and Point Four have been more recently attacked.

I sent the report to Washington as directed. A few weeks later I was overwhelmed to find my name, in connection

with items of the report (which was highly classified), head-
lined in the Shanghai papers. Someone in Washington had
given the gist of the matter to the United Press, which
released the story throughout the world. I must confess that
after the initial shock, my reaction was one of pleasure. The
report was honest and objective. Its release could only mean
a change in policy, perhaps a promotion for me.

But I was very naïve indeed. At the direction of General
Marshall, who had become Secretary of State, Walton Butterworth, our Minister in Shanghai, sent me a most insulting
telegram, accusing me of insubordination and of maliciously
adding to the friction between the United States and Russia. Butterworth knew, having seen and passed on to me the
original cable, that I had only obeyed a directive. He knew
that I, in Shanghai without a copy of the report in my possession (security forbade the retention of duplicates of such
reports), could not possibly have had anything to do with
the release of the report in Washington. But I had committed
the then unpardonable sin of reporting something that would
hurt the feelings of the Communists.

A few hours after I had heard from Butterworth in Nanking, a cable came from Washington. Again blandly dis-
regarding all the facts in the case, the cable (signed by Marshall) began, in the timeworn vocabulary of such cables:
"The Department has been seriously embarrassed by. . . ."
I was stripped of all authority to make further studies or
reports and was forced to clear all future work through a
third secretary in Nanking. The climax came that very night
when I heard myself denounced by Radio Moscow as a war-
monger! Moscow and Washington were singing in complete
harmony as far as I was concerned.

In passing, it is of interest to note that during the last year
I have received a number of copies of *The China Review*,
published in Shanghai, as I have already mentioned, by Bill
Powell, his wife, and several other Americans. Surely one of
the most anti-American publications in the world today, this

magazine has carried such stories as "Atrocities in Korea" (with a double spread of pictures including one of a mass grave in which, it was said, the bodies of ten thousand Korean men, women, and children, killed by brutal American troops, had been found by Chinese "volunteers"); "Drive Against Spies and Saboteurs"; "U. S. Spy Ring Smashed in Peiping"; and "U. S. War Against China." Such titles indicate the communist line I pointed out in my ill-advised report of '46. It was just that I had been unforgivably premature. Needless to say the promotion for which I had hoped was not forthcoming.

I returned to Korea, laden with some of the procommunist literature I found everywhere in Shanghai. (One book on Korea, written by British communist correspondents, I had captured from the desk of the director of the U. S. Information Service.) I found Korea more than usually disrupted with a deluge of rumors pertaining to America's part in the new order. Survey teams from Washington came and went, planning the State Department's Korean operation. All of us received questionnaires asking if we would be interested in staying on in Korea with the new American mission which was to take the place of Military Government. Some said there would be only a few score employed to advise the new Korean Government; others reported that a vast new organization, perhaps numbering in the thousands, would emerge from the uncertainty. It was a time of little work and of much speculation about new working conditions, living conditions, and salaries.

The Provincial Military Government Groups first felt the change, as property long occupied by American units was turned over to Korean owners, and as American advisors were pulled in to Seoul to await the outcome or to receive immediate reassignment to Japan, Okinawa, or Guam. Elsie and I were among the last to leave Chunchon. After much argument I had persuaded the interim authorities to appoint one young American civilian to take our place. Of course,

Hong Shin and Pak Chung Young remained, so we felt the work of the shrine would continue in good hands.

As old faces left, new faces came in from Washington to organize the new American Mission in Korea, known soon as AMIK to Americans and Koreans alike. The story of AMIK is an important one because to a large extent it is the story of postwar American embassies abroad. And to express the feeling of the times it is not possible to tell the story of AMIK in strictly chronological terms. Rather it must be told in terms of individuals in Seoul and Washington, of the programs and projects they directed; and it must be told also in terms of the way we lived and in terms of our relations to the people and the government of the world's newest sovereign state.

Take, for instance, Ralph Bricker, the man who on that Sunday in June, many months later, was to urge in vain that steps be taken to save millions of dollars worth of U. S. Government property. Ralph Oliver Bricker arrived during the early days of AMIK to become deputy director of the Joint Administrative Services (known to the American colony as JAS); he later became its director. The job was a tremendous one and was never anything but heartbreak and worry. If Bricker had not been a man of great good humor and huge physique, a man who loved hard work, hunting, and fishing with equal passion, he would have sunk under the weight of complaints, Washington directives and counterdirectives, and of his own qualms of conscience for the careless waste and still more careless greed that characterized some of his fellow countrymen. Because, as it turned out, we were to fight the menace of communism with the tools of materialism.

For the most part, post-Occupation Americans in Seoul lived in one or another of the embassy hotels (Traymore, Capitol, Banto, Naija, Chisan, Kukje, Yongsan) or in one of the 375 private homes owned by the American Government and scattered throughout the city in little graftings of American suburbia, from Yung-dung-po to the North Gate. The days of poor quarters, of no electricity or water or heat, were practically over. It soon became apparent that AMIK would take care of its own, offering the best available regardless of cost.

The hotels were well equipped with bars and lounges. Two had roof gardens. The season's first dinner dance was always scheduled for the roof of the Naija Hotel. The houses naturally varied somewhat in style and luxury, but all were completely furnished, were rent free, and were supplied with two servants on the payroll of the United States Government. (In the very early days of AMIK, three servants were granted, but Bricker was able to reduce the number to two, thus saving several thousand dollars each month.) Over and above these advantages, there was free telephone and taxi service for Americans; household repairs (plumbing, electrical, even repapering and repainting) were taken care of at government expense; and shops consisting of PX, beauty parlor, barber shop, liquor store, etc., were available to the Americans. Liquor, gasoline, and the articles at the PX (ranging from cigarettes to suits for the men and dresses for the women) were tax free. After all, Seoul was listed as a "hardship post" in Washington.

It must be admitted that Ralph Bricker did what he could. When he inherited his little empire, it included some eight thousand Korean employees who shared in none of the afore-mentioned advantages and received salaries scarcely sufficient for survival, even lower than was being paid by Korean industry. Bricker was able to reduce this number to five thousand, in the teeth of the anguished cries of the master race. After cutting the number of free servants from three to two (more cries!), he turned down the easily requested, and formerly just as easily granted, repaint jobs on the front parlor or new gardens to insure privacy. He even had the audacity to limit the free use of taxis. Here and there, in other words, he had begun to save the taxpayer's money.

As for the five thousand Korean employees of the embassy who were not fired, the contrast between their economic and social status and that of the American employees of the embassy was a serious handicap to our being accepted in Korea as an unmitigated blessing. There were occasions when two months or more would elapse between pay envelopes. The official attitude seemed to be that it could hardly matter whether the "gooks" were paid or not since they were by nature dishonest, stupid, and somewhat subhuman. The highest salary was the equivalent of sixteen dollars a month. (This was far better than under the Army, so we had made some progress.)

Ralph Bricker and I had managed against odds to produce fairly decent wages for our USIS employees, on a sliding cost-of-living scale that might help meet Seoul's creeping inflation. It was remarkable to see the decrease in stealing as soon as the new wage scale went into effect. Americans the world over seem slow to realize the connection between hunger and dishonesty. In countries where poverty is the order of the day, people live from meal to meal. When there is not enough for the next, they are bound to steal. When it comes to what any of us would do for survival, we live in glass houses!

During the first year no effort was made to give Koreans vacation privileges equal to those of the American staff, although I believe the law provides that *all* employees of the U. S. Government be given vacations with pay. Again, after considerable trouble and effort, Ralph Bricker and John Sinclair (personnel officer) obtained a two-week annual leave with pay for all Korean employees. But sick leave with pay, a right of other government workers, was never granted to them. It is a wonder, in the light of this "democratic" treatment of our co-workers, that more did not go over to the Communists when the North Korean Army entered Seoul. Actually, the percentage was relatively low.

The embassy did provide physical examinations for all Korean employees, not for the benefit of the employee, but to protect us from contamination. These examinations included complete laboratory and blood tests, which gave, I think, a clue to one of Asia's great problems. Of the three hundred employees of the U. S. Information Service who received laboratory tests, nearly 90 per cent were found to be infected with intestinal worms. Many of us who have lived in the Orient know what it means. In those long infected it produces extreme languor and malaise. How often, I wonder, is the lazy, stupid "gook" neither lazy nor stupid but a victim of such parasites.

But in spite of the problems of the five thousand Korean employees, the two hundred Americans Bricker had inherited from his poker-playing predecessor (who had his favorites at court, and not always those with the most savory reputations) were an even tougher matter to deal with. One of them had been implicated in construction graft. Another was suspected of bringing liquor through the Korean customs for the sake of a business crony. A few others were tarred with the brush of black marketing, smuggling, and the sale of U. S. Government equipment. One difficult case was that of a man who was completely illiterate yet who was receiving a $6,000 salary in a position of importance, a man still in the Foreign Service and recently recommended for a new $8,000 post.

Since many of the American staff had been transferred directly from the Army of Occupation in Korea, there had been a shocking lack of proper screening, and scant attention had been given to the capabilities of the particular individual for holding a particular job. There were five men, in positions of considerable importance, who had not even been checked for security eighteen months after the reorganization. The number of misfits, security risks, and incompetents, not to mention alcoholics and homosexuals, was something to write home about—if one could have expected an answer. Bricker tried, to the best of his ability, to weed

out and reassign the more destructive and harmful characters under his jurisdiction. But before he could get very far,
somebody cut the 38th Parallel. That ended that.

It is quite true that people abroad are prone to let go, being
far from native haunts where their behavior might be seen
and judged. This tendency is greatly increased when they
are free to live beyond themselves on the generosity of the
American taxpayer. I cannot believe it to be true, that the
only way to get good men into foreign service is to pay
them bigger and better salaries, provide them with electric
kitchens in Nairobi. I cannot believe that the spiritual senses
of the men and women of the United States have become so
dulled by materialism that they are impervious to the call of
responsibility, of honor, of courage, which are demanded by
the hazards and adventures of this new kind of pioneering.

In spite of the fact that the 375 homes owned and leased
by the embassy were for the most part the best homes in
Seoul, many families were not pleased with them. Some had
been built by the Army, but most had been occupied by the
Japanese businessmen and officials who once ruled the city.
They were Japanese style, with mat *tatami* floors, sliding
paper doors and windows, and Japanese toilets and baths.
Certain charms, certain inconveniences, went hand in hand.
Heating was often a problem, and the water supply was at
times extremely erratic. But while whole sections of Seoul
went lightless, Americans had constant electricity from the
huge generators in each large residential area. One could be
comfortable quite easily, and with interior decorating the
homes could be made very attractive.

Sixty members of the American Mission earned in excess
of $10,000 annually, and they were often the ones who most
vociferously demanded houses "in line with their position."
A certain wife, finding her assigned house had been occupied
previously by an American of Korean ancestry, insisted on
leaving it. Another requested that the embassy purchase a
vacant lot next to her house in order to have a buffer zone

between her child and the young of Korea. And since houses were assigned according to salary and length of service, with salary taking precedence, there were howls of disapproval from the old-timers—and why not?

Korea is one of the most beautiful countries of the world, with a history well worth exploration by scholar and traveller alike. It had roads of sorts that led to beautiful temples, monasteries, beaches, and quaint, walled cities. Yet few of the Americans stationed in Seoul ever went outside the city. Too many of them spent their leisure hours (and, with servants, almost every hour was leisure) finding fault with the situation.

If Americans had been more eager to see the country and take part in Korean life, they would have had less time for worrying about themselves and drowning their worries in alcohol. Most recreation centered around the embassy bars. Every Wednesday and Saturday evening, huge cocktail parties were regularly scheduled. The consumption of liquor was terrific, and illness and absenteeism due to it became a constant problem.

It also created a strained and unhealthy situation with respect to the Korean officials who, like all Orientals, were concerned with face and felt they had to keep up with the Joneses by giving equally lavish brawls. But liquor was not tax free to Koreans, as it was to us, and the expense of entertaining several hundred thirsty Americans at one party was prohibitive. President Rhee was finally forced to order all Korean officials to entertain only with Coca-Cola and cookies. Bricker tried to have the ambassador call off the Wednesday and week-end gaiety, but to no avail. Reports of the overindulgence finally seeped through to Washington, and an investigation started. The Foreign Service inspector assigned to an on-the-spot inspection spent several months in Seoul and was duly entertained. On one memorable occasion he passed out in the Ambassador's parlor. But he reported he saw no evidence of excessive drinking.

In an attempt to break up the huddle of drinking and malicious gossip in Seoul, some of us, including Ralph Bricker and John Sinclair, thought of a way to inveigle Americans into the country where they were so loathe to go. (For one thing, they had been inclined to believe Washington's "post report" that Korean roads were impassable for cars.) We came up with Taechun Beach, 135 miles south of Seoul.

Missionaries, at the end of the last century, had discovered a lovely beach at Sorai and had developed it as a resort. But Sorai now lay north of the Parallel. Wonsan, another fine beach on the east coast, is also above the 38th, and the mountain resort at Chiri-san, near Pusan, was in constant danger of attack by communist guerillas. Therefore it was necessary to develop another spot, and Taechun seemed perfect. The Methodist, Presbyterian, and Seventh Day Adventist missions had contributed funds for that purpose, and in the summer of '49 a lodge was built. By the next spring some twenty private cottages had sprung up. Although not of the missionary group, I was allowed to buy a lot and build a tiny Korean-style beach house at a total cost of $500.

Our hope that official Americans would take advantage of the opportunities at Taechun Beach proved a dismal failure. One reason was that the missionaries, for whom Taechun had become a favorite place for vacation and study, were not fond of embassy morals. The Protestant church in Korea is strict and legalistic. Drinking, smoking, and travel or business on Sunday are frowned upon by Korean Christian leaders. The missionaries obviously did not welcome an invasion of American officials. It was therefore suggested that the embassy lease property farther along the three-mile beach. The total cost would have been about a thousand dollars to renovate some deteriorating Japanese summer homes. Violent opposition put the scheme on the shelf. And the communist invasion reduced the argument to an academic one.

AMIK, and its component parts—the embassy proper, the Economic Cooperation Administration, the Joint Administrative Services, the Korean Military Advisory Group, and the United States Information Service—totaled some fifteen hundred Americans, ranging from billet managers, menu planners, and butchers, to high-ranking Foreign Service career officers, expert engineers, and radio and information specialists. In all probability Seoul was the only place in the world where "butchers, bakers and candlestick makers" were honored with diplomatic status.

Yet, ours *was* a really important mission. It was our responsibility to help a fledgling nation to its feet, to help build its economy and its political structure, and to arm it sufficiently to protect what we had assisted in building. AMIK was also an important experiment for the State Department, for it was one of the first, and certainly the largest, of the "coordinated missions" where all parts of the American program were united under one head and for one purpose. It is unfortunate that we lived in isolation from the people we were there to help, for we thereby cut ourselves off from the essential knowledge of what was going on behind the scenes with the Koreans, North and South alike.

The men and women of AMIK were not all incompetent by any means. There were intelligent and earnest people in all parts of the program: men like Bricker and Mathews of the Joint Administrative Services; like Bunce, Baldridge, Kinney, Fisher, and Leveau of ECA; like the young career officers who did their best to reach beyond the walls of AMIK and to find out what the Koreans were thinking and what was going on to the north.

Now that it is too late, we realize the tragic consequences of the policy of "isolationism" in our embassies the wide world over. In Asia today, it is not enough to give aid and train armies. We must not only give rifles to the democratic new armies. We must somehow reach the hearts of men and women and make them willing to use the rifles in the defense of their homes, willing to fight on our side. It is a tremendous undertaking and one which is doomed to tragic failure until the bureaucratic red tape in Washington is unsnarled and we get down to human beings.

Chapter 7

Washington Background

THE State Department information program for Korea had been planned in Washington in July 1948, six months before the turnover from Army. At the time, it was agreed that Korea should have a staff of twenty-four American information and cultural specialists. (Later the number was increased to thirty-four, the largest American staff maintained anywhere overseas by the Voice of America.) During the election of 1948 the staff of Army information specialists had been greatly increased, and some members who wished to stay on and who were considered of high enough calibre were automatically transferred to the new "permanent" program. Much work had to be done before the actual transfer, since the Department of State does not recognize Defense Department security clearances and all personnel had to be rescreened.

Yet the wheels within wheels in the Department's machinery moved so slowly that by December 31, the day before the official transfer, not a single person had received a commitment of employment. Meanwhile man after man, originally interested in staying, had altered his plans and taken advantage of free Army transportation to return home. Thirteen of us had remained, on faith alone, because the Department of State had not even been able to decide on salary levels.

It was only after a series of frantic cables and tele-conversations that salaries were finally agreed upon for the "lucky thirteen" and we were able to begin building a new information structure with half the proposed State Department staff and with a fourteenth of the Army staff we had formerly had. The situation became critical a few months later when the Department reneged on its commitments, deciding that most of the thirteen were being overpaid, and cut salaries back retroactively to January 1. This obviously did not help morale in a situation already uncertain and muddled.

Meanwhile, an unbearable load was placed on our little band of survivors. I was deputy director of the new U. S. Information Service in Korea and acted as chief of all operations. It was incumbent upon me to supervise the ten provincial information centers scattered from Kaesong and Chunchon to Pusan, since none of the centers any longer had resident American personnel (the State Department theory being that Americans should work only in a nation's capital or a few large cities rather than in the country where they might be absorbed by the people). It was necessary for me to handle all financing and supply. I was overseer of some three hundred Korean employees for whom I had to write very complete job descriptions in Foreign Service terms. I also wrote the heightened reports so dear to the hearts of Washington bureaucracy. And I tried, betwixt and between, to do a little original work in the information field at a time when I felt it was strategically needed. My requests for stenographic help being denied, I was my own secretary and typist. Elsie handled my files as a necessary extra, over and above her loaded schedule.

At the same time, our physical needs seemed a matter of no concern to the department. No arrangements at all had been made to equip and supply the branch operations or even to pay the Korean personnel in such distant places as Pusan, Taejon and Chunchon. After the employees had gone without salaries for two months (a major tragedy for many of our people who led a hand-to-mouth existence), I carried the money to them myself. A payroll trip took at least five days, and more often a week, on the Korean railroads. I traveled in a baggage car, equipped with a camp stove and cot, and spent endless hours in lonely freight yards or being shunted from train to train. All the money I carried with me was in cash (some five million *won*), and I stood by while each employee received his few thousand and signed his pay-roll forms. Later, when the burden became too great, Elsie made some of the expeditions for me, carrying as much as a million *won* by jeep to the 38th Parallel information centers. We gave up this hazardous procedure when we heard rumors of a plot to waylay her.

There were questions of policy to be decided. The policy planning of the State Department was at variance with that of the Army. Under the Army we were allowed a great deal of local autonomy. We could, if we had the facilities, produce our own exhibits and motion pictures or develop projects "on location," as it were, for a given situation. We could do as we had done during the elections, when in a few short weeks we produced a full-length documentary film and millions of leaflets and were provided at the same time with the equipment to take our story directly to twenty million people.

It was obvious, from the day the State Department took over, that we would withdraw into Seoul and use other media than personal contacts to present ourselves and our program to the people of Korea. The gap between our country and theirs, which had been narrowed slightly by the valiant, if top-heavy and regulation-bound, efforts of the Army of Occupation, had already begun to widen once more. Our hope was to halt the trend, to gain approval for a program that would meet Korea's special problems, and to collect the right people and the right equipment to do ourselves proud. Because logistics are fully as important in carrying out a foreign policy as in conducting a military campaign, the right men and the right equipment should be in the right place at the right time. For this reason I was sent back to the States for ten days of consultations to persuade

Washington that we desperately needed help—and under-standing.

My trip was swift indeed. I took a Northwest Airlines plane direct from Seoul via the Aleutians to Washington. Because of the time change I was able to leave Seoul after lunch one day and have dinner in Minneapolis the next. As short as the time was, it was like stepping into another world.

I had spent little time in Washington since the summer of 1946. That summer, as chief of the Far East Area Division, I had been responsible for all of our information and cultural expansion in the Far East. Since then, several reorganizations of the State Department had taken place, and I hoped that the general atmosphere had changed. Instead, I stepped right into another very thorough shake-up. These reorganizations are periodic. It is evidently believed they will allay public suspicion and criticisms of the department. Another reorganization, one to end all reorganizations, was completed in 1952!

It was amusing to see the same old faces pop up in new positions or in old positions with new names. When I was in Washington in 1946, a special study had been made of the whole informational and cultural program. The study had been made by a group of efficiency experts from Chicago, and their report was detailed and to the point. I had opportunity to see it just before I left Washington, and I know that a number of officials had been singled out for severe criticism, with unmistakable suggestions that their services be terminated. To my surprise, these men were still much in evidence, quite ready to help me with my Korean problems.

Most disquieting of all, I found that the Foreign Service officer in charge of the new Far Eastern reorganization was one John Melby. Melby, when assigned to Moscow during the war, made a special trip with Russian officials to view the Katyn Forest massacre, and it was allegedly he who reported to Washington that it was obviously a German atrocity. It

ELSIE CALDWELL ADDRESSING 38TH PARALLEL CROWD FROM JEEP TOP

Seoul, 1950

AFTERMATH—THE CALDWELL HOME, 1952

AFTERMATH—SEOUL, 1952

was Melby who, with no experience in the field of propaganda, was given the supervision of all such activities of the State Department in China during the Marshall mission's effort to force a coalition government on Chiang. He refused to allow USIS to send the American story into the communist-controlled areas of China. He argued that we should work with the supposed middle-of-the-roaders in China, most of whom have since turned out to be full-fledged Communists. It was Melby who approved a project for sending Chinese communist students to study in America, a project also approved by General Marshall. (The students were selected and were in Shanghai waiting for transportation when the Nationalist Government put its foot down and refused them exit permits.) It was Melby who was assigned to rewrite the truthful reports which Ambassador J. Leighton Stuart had written so that Washington would know what was actually happening in China during those crucial months. Melby's record showed a remarkable blindness to communist methods and aims, and yet it was he who was given the responsibility of supervising our military aid to southeast Asia in 1949 and 1950.

Was it surprising, then, to find so little real interest in, or understanding of, our moral commitment to develop, build up, and defend Korea? I was asked time and again: "Why the fuss about Korea? Why is it important?" But at the same time that I was answering these questions I was fending off new and expensive projects. Korea was a bureaucrat's dream, a virgin territory in which to set up an operation with all the wonderful job opportunities attached. One particular project involved a long and acrimonious policy meeting. The department was publishing a beautiful Russian-language magazine called *Amerika*. The group in the information office backing *Amerika* saw in Korea an opportunity to expand. *Amerika* should be made available to Koreans! I could see no sense in this. A publication of such magnificence and expense would be out of place in Korea. Furthermore, we were already publishing a less ambitious monthly magazine in Seoul, and it seemed sufficient. The argument was settled by delegating one of the staff members of *Amerika* to take a quick trip by air (cost, round trip, $1,800) to Seoul to check our publication. The young lady who got the assignment actually proved quite helpful in many ways, but the incident is typical. Anyone even remotely interested fought for a share of the program, regardless of the over-all picture.

The Korean information budget was a new budget as far as the department was concerned. Before January 1, 1949, the Army had paid for the program in Korea. A new operation overseas naturally brings with it new possibilities for adding personnel in Washington. A large part of the budget hearings and meetings among department personnel were spent in determining how many new positions would be necessary to backstop us in Korea. We had originally hoped for twenty-four information people, including administrative and stenographic help. The department experts raised this to thirty-four by adding some fascinating new projects and programs. At the same time, in order to backstop, supervise, and supply these thirty-four, a total of *thirty-six* new positions were added in Washington. I pointed out that this didn't look well, particularly when the whole ECA operation in Korea, responsible for spending $150,000,000, was backstopped by just twelve people. A small reduction was finally accomplished over the anguished protests of the divisions which were cut.

One of the projects involved establishing a very large English Teaching Institute in Seoul. The staff was to consist of eight American teachers, and English was to be taught by the recently developed method known as phonemics. The institute would require a great deal of expensive equipment and an entire building. Although none of us had asked for it, this expansion had already been approved and some of the personnel employed. Knowing of Seoul's serious building shortage (every building the American Government used was taken from Koreans and meant one less for them), I telephoned the embassy in Seoul to warn it and to point out the necessity of locating a building before personnel and equipment began to arrive. The program got off to a very bad start in Washington. Before I left, the professor who had been hired to direct it arrived for his indoctrination, shots, travel arrangements, etc. The department had run the usual security check on him but had somehow missed a little larceny in the gentleman's background. He was arrested in a Washington hotel room some days before he was to embark for Korea and the battle for democracy.

As I wandered through the maze of department red tape, bickering, and politics during those sad two weeks, I was again aware how little the average American knows about his Department of State and its operation. I believe it is the least understood department of our government. Every farmer comes in contact with the Department of Agriculture. The Treasury Department and the Departments of the Interior and Justice play an appreciable and visible part in American lives. The Post Office Department comes right to our doors. Yet the Department of State, which, when all is said and done, can make for war or peace and which is responsible for the intelligent handling of our foreign affairs, is a closed book to the man in the street, even to Congress.

It was this Department, so little in touch with the great human reservoir it represents, which had the immense task of explaining our way of life to the Koreans, and of learning theirs. To a foreigner, it is the Foreign Service of our Department of State, from humblest clerk to ambassador, which stands for America. I have become convinced, from my experiences in China and Korea, that that clerk or stenographer is in the final analysis more important than the Secretary of State or even the President. In his or her daily life, the clerk or stenographer will make friends or enemies for America. Regardless of the merit of our product, the final acceptance of it will depend upon the people who carry it abroad.

For the past two years there have been over ten thousand men and women in our Department of State's world-wide information program, with a total of close to thirty thousand in all the divisions of the department's activities at home and abroad. To these can be added other thousands employed by ECA (now Mutual Security Administration) and the new Point Four program. All of these men and women, regardless of the kitty from which they are paid, are members of the department's Foreign Service; they have Foreign Service ranks and are subject to the regulations and procedures of the service. One of the most serious mistakes of the department is the failure to realize the importance of this vast number of people as individuals and to impress upon them the inevitable consequences of their individual actions. Enormous attention is paid to policy, with little conception that people *are* policy. Far from being representative of American democracy in operation, the department is a honeycomb of bureaucratic regimentation and protocol. Too often the product turned out by the machine has lost both its human value and its quality of being American.

Take an example. Before a new motion picture goes abroad, it has run the gamut of a dozen policy conferences. The script is examined by regional specialists. The finished picture is again reviewed. Certain officers of the department are paid eight to ten thousand dollars a year to do nothing more than preview movies. The consequent delay in getting the film to its destination (in our case, Korea) can well be imagined. Often the need that led to making the film in the first place has evaporated. There is not the least interest in the man overseas who is going to show the film, if he ever gets it. This man is more often than not an officer with no training at all in the language, customs, history, or temperament of the country in which he is serving. He may, and probably does, have the "gook" philosophy. He may be an alcoholic or a homosexual, or he may, as has happened in several cases, have a criminal record. But his security clearance, which has taken from six months to a year, has proved that he is not a Communist. And even Communists have slipped by.

The security clearance has taken so long that now the fellow gets an accelerated "training" of two or three weeks. He listens to a lecture or two on the country to which he is assigned. He is told to consult the "country file" in a row of filing cabinets bursting with paper. He spends one or two days cooling his heels in certain offices, waiting for a VIP to look up from his desk and greet him. He gets a thorough briefing in departmental protocol—how his calling cards are to be engraved, at whose doors he is to drop the cards, and in what order. Then he is flown to his post at considerable expense.

If he is a typical American who has never traveled in the Orient (and most often he is) he is immediately shocked to the eyebrows by the poverty, the absence of plumbing, the filth, the strange and awful food, the beggars, and the "jibberish" spoken around him. He judges the people according to his degree of shock, and then retreats into the closed circle of American club-bar-cocktail society. In all his orientation he has never heard a word about the real implications of the vast war of ideologies of which he is to be a part; he hears no talk of the privilege it should be to serve his country, nor the responsibilities such a service entails.

In selecting him, the department has made no effort to test his adaptability or to find out if he wants to fit into the life of a strange and foreign land. For a man going to the Far East, the situation is particularly tragic. The short training that is given him takes place among men and women in the department's Far Eastern Sections who, for the most part, were once employed by the Institute of Pacific Relations or closely allied agencies. Whether from misjudgment or conspiracy, these officers have long thought of communism in the Far East as a logical development of movements towards independence, without connection with the Moscow network.

Without previous training, without previous experience

outside the United States, with no particular incentive to learn about the new country (if he studies the language it must be on his own time), with every emphasis placed upon social life within the tightly-knit embassy or consulate circle, with never an inkling of what political forces are at work in his own or any other country, what wonder that the new Foreign Service officer falls quickly and securely into the routine of embassy life, sees little or nothing of the people or the country, and adopts that unmistakable attitude of superiority which plays so easily into communist accusations that we are a country bent solely on imperialism abroad. By the very nature of the establishment built by Joint Administrative Services in Korea, this tragedy was compounded.

It reminded me of the many trips Elsie and I had taken to beautiful Kangwha Island, off the mouth of the Han River. Along the shores of this island is a wall, built centuries ago by the Korean kings who retreated behind it while the armies of neighboring China overran all the rest of Korea. The king and his court lived there in safety and isolation for many many years, until the invasion rolled back northward and it was safe to emerge into the outside world again. I thought of the walls we built around us in Seoul and other parts of the world and wondered whether, in our isolation from the friends we had come to help, our walls would also give us safety or only the tragic illusion of it.

Last year the Department of State said it was appointing a commission to determine how religion could be injected into the information program. It seems to me that such studies are unnecessary. Well trained, adaptable, sympathetic men and women who believe in America bring with them a religion that any native can recognize. If they are not shackled by old, outmoded departmental regulations they can succeed where all the motion pictures, libraries, and radio programs money can buy will fail. Conversely, even the best informational and cultural material we produce will not be effective unless it is carried by individual Americans who realize their responsibilities and who know their work.

Even good men in the field must have considerate and effective administrative support at home. But though the Department of State has mushroomed in recent years, its increase in personnel has not resulted in improved administrative techniques. Again, this is due largely to preoccupation with that magic word *policy*.

Before any cable or letter can be sent abroad, it must be initialed by some representative of every division or unit of the department which is even remotely touched by the content. In one of the department buildings are several women who aggregate almost one hundred years of government service, and no message, no matter how urgent, can escape their vigilance until the proper initials have been applied. A man in Shanghai may have a dying wife in Boston, but the message authorizing an emergency leave home cannot go out unless it has been initialed by: (1) the Bureau of Far Eastern Affairs; (2) the Division of Chinese Affairs; (3) the office of personnel; (4) the budget and fiscal office; (5) the travel section; (6) the office of the particular program to which he is attached—six sets of initials, and then the signature of the Secretary of State himself.

Since only certain individuals have the authority to initial, and since that person may be out, ill, or on annual leave, and since a week end or holiday may intervene, it can be hours, even days, before a cable is dispatched. If a telegram is to be sent quickly, many a ten-thousand-dollar-a-year man, rather than submit it to the far from tender mercies of messenger boys walks it around from office to office himself to obtain the necessary clearances more rapidly.

Sometimes the results of the system are amusing. On one occasion, while chief of the China Branch of the USIS program, I was also coordinator of various phases of the whole Far Eastern program. In the latter capacity I wrote an important cable to China, initialed it, and started it on its way. One week later the cable came back for me to initial again in my capacity as chief of the China Branch!

Supplies take months, sometimes years, to reach their destinations; policy decisions that should be made in hours require days; dispatches and letters remain unanswered; salary payments are sometimes months in arrears. Inefficiency of this kind cannot fail to effect the morale of distant men and women who have no way to call for help and are put in humiliating situations by such delays.

The department is often inconsistent and unjust in its personnel practices: a young man wanted desperately to be employed by the Voice of America in China but failed to be taken. He spoke Chinese and seemed an ideal choice. He was turned down because he had been stationed in a communist country during the war, when in the United States Army. He had never for a moment espoused the communist cause; his record was excellent. Yet he was rejected by the department. On the other hand, there are career officers in the department who have actively preached the Chinese communist cause to such an extent that they since have been brought under investigation and even arrest; and they have steadily risen in position. It has become axiomatic that a career officer can do no wrong. As Robert Bendiner said in his book *The Riddle of the State Department*, published ten years ago, "It is an achievement to get into the Foreign [career] Service, it is even more of a feat to be dismissed." He knew of only one career officer asked to resign.

For the non-career men who form a large part of the Foreign Service, it is a different story. Many are turned down or dismissed for very slight reasons, such as a nervous breakdown of many a year ago or knowing the wrong modern language (one young man was turned down because, besides English, he knew only Japanese). The department uses its broad powers of dismissal without hearings to weed out nonconformists more often than communist sympathizers. Hew to the department line, or else.

A premium is placed upon caution, since wrong guesses mean black marks. A creed of snobbery, self-protection, and conservatism has been developed in the men of the old school who actually run the department. If a man holds high enough position himself, or has friends who do, he can be an alcoholic, a degenerate, a neurotic, a black marketeer, or smuggler. For the Department of State, though relatively immune to outside political influence, is afire with internal politics chiefly fostered by the old-line career men.

On the credit side, one can see changes for the better taking place. Not many years ago the Foreign Service officer paid for transportation abroad of personal effects. Salaries were very low. Now even the least paid clerk is allowed twenty thousand pounds of free baggage. A few years ago, those who had no private funds found it difficult to raise a family and faced retirement with little or no savings.

Today the pendulum has swung the other way. There are hundreds of men and women making more money in Foreign Service than they ever could in private enterprise. Now it is only the lowest grades in the career service that are underpaid. It wasn't long ago that an officer who became ill overseas might be forced to pay his own medical bills. Today there are dispensaries, doctors, and nurses in our larger missions, and bills for illness incurred in line of duty are paid by the government.

At one time, a man could remain indefinitely in a desolate or unhealthy post. Now he is given statutory leave every two years. Today, one whole unit of the department is devoted to the welfare of its officers and employees overseas. Automobiles, refrigerators, furniture, even sports equipment are purchased wholesale and shipped to posts on every continent. In fact, the danger now is that the department spends a disproportionate share of its time and money on seeing that employees are afforded the best that America can offer, no matter where they are assigned.

But to return to my two weeks in Washington in that spring of 1949. I had hoped in particular to locate some really competent persons, perhaps men who had served in Korea during the Occupation and already knew the country and its needs. I hoped, too, for approval of some of the autonomous projects which we had been allowed to develop under the Army and which had helped to keep us in close touch with the people. Unfortunately, the so-called expert's report that Korea had no roads still dogged our efforts, and would not mobile motion-picture units therefore be useless? Having driven from one side of the country to the other, I finally succeeded in having ten suitable units ordered. I scanned many a motion picture and selected a few good titles; but I argued strenuously for permission to continue the making of films in Seoul, believing, as I still do, that pictures concerned with local problems and with local actors speaking their own language and acting in their own environments will always be more effective than the most lavish Hollywood production.

Little was accomplished in the way of finding good personnel. One man I wanted was considered too pro-Syngman Rhee, and secretarial and clerical help was unobtainable at the time. Months afterward, when it was too late, the help began suddenly to arrive. Anyway, the unexpected $3,000,-000 budget was merrily approved, even without proper tools or suitable manpower to make effective use of it. I went back to Korea somewhat confused but glad to be back in a land where issues were clear and things seemed to make sense.

Chapter 8

The Voice That Failed

AS I HAVE said before, the American Mission in Korea was the largest State Department mission abroad. It was the largest administrative operation overseas. It contained the largest U. S. Information Service. Although it was several months after my return to Seoul before we became largest in staff, our USIS operation was already immense in scope —so immense and varied that within a few days after my return from Washington a special mission of five persons, including the young lady from *Amerika*, arrived from the department to study our activities. Three of the men spent some time with us trying honestly to see our problems. The fourth, the officer in charge of all information activities in the Far East, arrived on a Saturday afternoon and left Monday morning. He seemed put out at having to come to Korea at all and was obviously anxious to return to Washington to protect his interests in the current reorganization.

I spent two weeks showing our visitors our operations and explaining our many problems. In particular I was anxious to impress upon them the importance of keeping up our rural activities throughout South Korea, which is, after all, 80 per cent rural in population. We were still maintaining our Army-established information centers in each province; and as part of our indoctrination program for the visitors, we took them up to Chunchon to spend the day at the shrine.

Hong Shin and Pak had a fine program going, and the visitors were duly impressed by the beauty of Peacock Mountain and the scope of our activities. After lunch we told

Hong that we would like to take our visitors up the Short Russia road and give them a look at no man's land along the Parallel. It had been months since I had been near the border. We drove up, not in the usual jeep, but in my brand-new PX car which had arrived in Seoul while I was in Washington. As we approached the road block at the bridge crossing the North Han River we stopped with the intention of taking pictures and relaxing over coffee before turning back, when we found ourselves under a sudden machine gun attack. This was the incident mentioned in Chapter 4. We were fortunate to escape with our lives.

This attack was immediately reported to the ambassador who, to my surprise, did not consider it of sufficient importance to report to Washington. Indeed, his desire was to keep the whole thing secret, especially from American newspaper correspondents in Korea. So for weeks I had to make peculiar explanations to friends who remarked upon the unusual holes in my new car.

But in one sense this terrifying episode should have been a lesson to us. I could not, if I had tried, have staged a better demonstration of the fact that we in South Korea were on the front lines, that we were face to face with communism and needed all the support we could get from home, physical as well as moral.

Our government had just announced that the last American troops, a regimental combat team, would soon be withdrawn. In the past we had often been invited to leave. Now, with a somewhat unexpected reversal of sentiment, South Korea was seething with huge parades and demonstrations urging our troops to stay at least until the South Korean Army was strong enough to defend the country. The demonstrators shouted also for more arms and more help in training their army. Demonstrations took place in every major city in South Korea, and while many of the parades were arranged by the South Korean Government in an effort to focus attention on the country's predicament, there was a great deal of spontaneity among the marchers in the street. I also noted a new friendliness towards us wherever I went in those weeks, even in the smallest villages. The people seemed to be trying desperately to make a formerly unwelcome guest feel at home, to be asking him to stay longer lest disaster overtake them.

The demonstrations produced certain reactions in our embassy. Ambassador Muccio sent a note to the Korean Foreign Office, protesting that the parades were blocking traffic in front of the embassy building. Then we had a special policy meeting. How could we counteract the Korean protests that we were not giving their armed forces the help we had promised? The result of that policy meeting was an order for the U. S. Information Service to distribute a series of news bulletins.

I was to discover, over a year later, that the bulletins, which went to every newspaper in South Korea, were absolutely false. In them we assured the people that America was, in fact, giving the Koreans immense military aid. We even listed over one hundred items of military equipment that had been delivered since the first of the year. We called attention to the Korean divisions our military advisors were training.

In point of fact, of the money appropriated by Congress, less than $20,000 worth of materials had been delivered by the time of the invasion. There were, it is true, a large number of items of equipment, but these consisted of telephone wire, field phones, etc. The real sinews of war were not delivered, but in our publicity we implied that it had been. In some cases, only one or two pieces of a particular item were delivered, but the item was listed as if delivered in bulk and useful quantity. Our answer to the Koreans was a lie, a barefaced lie which found us out a year later, in June 1950.

In spite of the fact that we were understaffed at the time, we were carrying on an enormous program. As deputy director of the United States Information Service, I was responsible for all our operations. My superior became more and more involved in writing speeches for the ambassador and in acting as a welcoming committee for visiting VIP's. Meanwhile, it seemed to me that USIS should continue the provincial operations that had helped so much to make the elections a success.

Under the Army we had established information centers not only in Chunchon but also in Kaesong, Seoul, Taejon, Taegu, Pusan, Chonju, Kwangju, Inchon, and on Cheju Island. I hoped that we would be able to continue all of these centers and that among the many Americans being recruited for us we would find men willing to work in the hinterland. Eventually, one man was approved for assignment to Pusan, South Korea's second largest city. The department and the ambassador could see no particular need of Americans in other localities. By the time of the invasion, when our staff had been increased to thirty-four, even the man in Pusan had been withdrawn into Seoul.

Operations at two of the provincial centers were abandoned, but through the Koreans we did continue the remaining nine centers. Our center in Seoul was probably the largest U. S. information center ever established. Occupying four floors of a building in the downtown district, it required the services of over one hundred Korean employees. The variety of activities we carried on and the quantity of material we produced and tried to disseminate, were impressive.

On the ground floor was a huge hall where the handsome exhibits, made up in Washington and changed every two weeks, were on display. On the second floor we had an auditorium where the motion-picture shows, concerts, lectures, and puppet shows were regularly presented. On the third floor was our eighteen-thousand-volume English-language library which carried, in addition to books, some two hundred American monthly magazines and periodicals. The latter included *The Atlantic Monthly*, *The Ceramics Journal*, *The Railway Age*, *Vogue*, etc. There were no publications in Korean other than our own USIS-published *American*

Monthly. A very large proportion of our books were in the field of advanced American economics and sociology. There were scores of scientific reference books costing from ten to twenty dollars a volume.

In spite of the fact that few Koreans could actually read our books and magazines, the libraries were extremely well attended, especially in the winter when the rooms were among the few warm spots in the city. But I believe there was another factor that attracted the large audience. In a country where paper was scarce and good books were either non-existent or out of reach because of cost, young students and intellectuals were glad just to handle the slick magazines and beautifully bound books and to gaze at pictures, even though they could not read the captions beneath.

At least the libraries did serve to demonstrate our library practice of free circulation. A reader could browse to his heart's content. This was revolutionary, for Korean libraries without exception still operated Japanese fashion: if one wished to see a book, even for a few moments, one asked an attendant who then unlocked the stacks long enough to bring the book out. I was warned we would have prohibitive losses when I decided to inaugurate an American-type loan service in an effort to further circulation. I realized the risk, but I felt that the books should be out in homes and classrooms if we were to reap any returns from such a large library investment.

I solved the problem by adopting the "guarantor" system.

In the Orient, a guarantor is part of both business and academic routine. A guarantor is one who recommends another and guarantees that the individual recommended will not steal and will make good. Following this pattern, our borrowers' cards carried a place where a guarantor signed, agreeing to pay for the book if it were lost or stolen. In time we were loaning hundreds of volumes and our annual loss was very small, only slightly above that experienced in any American library.

We also did our best to extend the use of the library by

loaning special collections of books on medicine, agriculture, and public health to professional societies and schools. Some of these were painstakingly translated and copied by hand for use as texts. In fact, a few good translations of a handful of technical know-how books, plus our best fiction, would have been worth more than all the thousands of English-language books we had on our shelves.

While our Seoul library was the largest in Korea, it was duplicated on a minor scale in all our other information centers. All in all, we had perhaps seventy-five thousand volumes, and several thousand American magazines and periodicals arrived each month. Our library operation was good— as good as such an operation can be in a country where hardly any English is spoken. But it was indicative of one of the failings of our American information program. The books and magazines we had in Seoul, in the shrine at Chunchon, or in Kaesong, were selected from the same list used in the selection of books for USIS libraries in Norway, or India, or South Africa. Little attention has been given to differing problems, rates of literacy, or knowledge of English. I can well understand that most of our books and magazines would be welcome in Scandinavian countries, but that fact did not make them equally worthwhile in Asia.

Our whole library operation, moreover, was crippled by home-side bureaucracy. Washington believes, perhaps with justification, that all USIS libraries abroad must be supervised and directed by professional librarians. We had two positions in our table of organization for these professionals. The position of library director called for a salary of $6,000 plus all the extras. I know something of the salary scale for librarians in America, and I know that many good librarians would jump for a chance at such a salary. The department, however, did not get around to filling the positions until just before the invasion.

Meanwhile our library was run, very efficiently if perhaps not according to the rules and regulations of the American

Library Association, by Margaret Christensen, a girl who had been transferred to us from an Army job. Chris came at a very low salary, and richly deserved something better. She was promised a raise when the Department of State took over, but she was among those whose salaries were cut back retroactively, after a promise of employment and salary had been given in writing. The department was unwilling to give her even a modest increase because she had no formal library training. The fact that she was doing the job and doing it well had no effect on the decision. Nor did our situation, made very difficult when she resigned in disgust, meet with any hurry-up action in sending us a replacement. The department could not supply us with a librarian. Neither would it let us keep the person who was doing the job.

In addition to the library, Washington sent us a deluge of photographic exhibits, pictorial displays of the best and most luxurious in American life, from clean well-stocked New England villages to the latest in housing developments. These exhibits were duplicated and sent out to the other centers. To some of them we were able to add photographs taken in Korea to show what America was trying to do there or to draw attention to similarities rather than differences between our countries.

On some days, in our Seoul information center, we had as many as ten thousand people. Statistically we were a great success. We kept a book in the lobby in which visitors could note their impressions and make suggestions. Occasionally the book turned up a crude communist slogan or threat, but many of the comments made sense. More and more the Koreans commented on the excellence of our pictures on life in America but asked, somewhat plaintively, for things that would help Korea. There we failed. Our portrayal of democracy in America was far over their heads. We also obviously missed another vital target, the heart. An exhibit on "low cost" housing, showing the Peter Stuyvesant Village project in lower Manhattan, simply cannot be of help to Koreans, struggling with mud and straw to solve their own housing problem.

The extent of our operations is not even partially reflected by the story of our library and exhibits. There were five weekly radio programs in Korean and relays of the Voice of America from New York. Quite often the locally produced shows, handled by Howell Teeple, were excellent, but for lack of radios in Korea the programs were heard only by a small minority in the larger cities. Moreover, most radios were made in Japan, and though they looked like American radios they were mere toys. They were useless in a matter of months, had no replacement parts available, and should not even have been mentioned in the statistical report on radio broadcasting in Korea.

USIS also operated the local Armed Forces radio station, WVTP, which broadcast entirely in English for the benefit of the American colony. WVTP featured all the programs so popular in America, our own pleasure in them being greatly increased by the fact that all the commercials had been deleted. The operation of WVTP by USIS was a violation of the spirit, and perhaps even of the laws (as passed by Congress) of our overseas information activities. It was patently operated for Americans, not Koreans. Eventually its operation required the full-time services of two of our small staff. Congress had appropriated the salaries of these men as information specialists with detailed responsibilities for bringing democracy to the Korean people.

This was not the only manner in which laws and regulations were flouted. USIS in Korea was a money-producing operation. Our *American Monthly* magazine was sold, its circulation eventually reaching forty thousand a month. In addition, our local motion-picture production unit (which made some of the few films worth showing) was selling its 35 mm. productions to the theaters of Korea. The income from these two operations soared into millions of Korean *won*, and of course both were in direct competition with similar Korean enterprises.

U. S. Government regulations specifically provide that any income from any source must immediately be reported and turned in to the United States Treasury. For months I tried to correct the irregularities arising from this anomalous situation. I believed it would be misunderstood by many Koreans. A primary American responsibility, as I saw it, was to teach the importance of honesty on the part of officials, to show that public funds should be accounted for in such a manner that there could be no criticism.

Instead, the above-mentioned funds were kept in Korean banks in the names of American individuals. I myself had a large sum in the Bank of Korea, and mine was but one of the three we kept in violation of law. When the money had been turned over to me, I was told that it was the residue of confidential funds entrusted to the Office of Civil Information and that as such no accounting need be made. It was many months before I discovered the real source of the money. At a time when our appropriations did not seem sufficient, an order had gone out to sell some twenty tons of government-owned newsprint. Newsprint was worth its weight in gold in Korea, and the sale brought in a very tidy sum.

These special accounts, certainly mine, were not used for the personal gain of any American. In the case of "my" money, we used it to pay for the hospital treatment of several employees, and to pay the salaries (in local currency) of several American employees whose employment approval was being delayed in the department. Of course, in doing this the embassy was violating another law, the one which specifically states that no one may be employed in the Department of State without a complete security check. We had three Americans on our payroll who, though in no manner disloyal, were being employed in violation of law.

The most unfortunate thing with regard to the special accounts was that unsavory gossip began circulating in Seoul. A large chunk of money had been spent by our director to finance the publication of leaflets which supposedly were being circulated in the Parallel areas. The general talk in

Seoul was that this money, with an accompanying gift of newsprint, had gone into the unsuccessful by-election campaign of a local politician. There is no doubt but that millions of *won* were spent on a variety of hazy projects without any accounting. It was an unhealthy situation for those of us who, like Caesar's wife, had always to remain completely above suspicion.

As for the *American Monthly*, it eventually had the largest paid circulation of any magazine in South Korea. It carried glamorously illustrated articles on various phases of life in the United States and translations of short stories and poetry. Ninety per cent of its readers were college students, which limited its circulation to a few large cities. For the educated minority it was a good magazine. For the average Kim and Pak of Korea it had much the same effect that *Fortune* magazine would have on a Mexican peon.

In addition to the films we made locally (dealing largely with ECA), we eventually began to receive a large number of titles from Washington. Perhaps one out of ten helped to meet the real needs of the Korean people. There was a lovely natural-color series on the national parks of America. When I found an awakening interest in democratic higher education, I requested a film on typical college life in America. The picture that came was called *UCLA* (University of California at Los Angeles). UCLA is one of our largest and best-equipped Universities. We had to show it to Korean students who studied all winter in barnlike unheated buildings with no textbooks, no laboratory equipment.

Motion pictures were given in all the information centers and by our mobile units whenever possible. Attendance mounted to as high as a million a month. None of the films was in any way remotely anticommunist. In fact, I do not believe there was one American film which even mentioned the word *Communist*.

On the other hand, we were able to enter the fight against communism in films locally produced. One of these, called

Brothers in Arms, was a gory epic of two brothers who fled from North Korea. Its purpose was to bring the Korean police and the Korean Army more closely together, to show that both services were for the benefit of the people. The film ended in a stirring fight against communist guerillas in the Chiri Mountains. Production of the film was held up for some time when department officials got wind of it. After some minor changes approval was granted and the film was a hit. How useful similar films would be in other parts of Asia today!

One of the greatest drains on the State Department abroad is a publication known as the *Wireless Bulletin.* It is broadcast to every USIS establishment in the world at tremendous expense. Being sent in Morse code, it requires code operators to pick it up. It must then be translated, after which it is edited, mimeographed, and distributed to newspapers free of charge. In Korea it took the time and energy of two Americans and a dozen Koreans, and it went to every newspaper in the country.

Occasionally the *Bulletin* carried condensed editorials from the *New York Times* and other newspapers of note in America. Once in a while there was an account of some activity of the state or federal governments. Now and then a statistical boast appeared: wheat production was so many per cent over the previous year. But for the most part the *Wireless Bulletin* contained the official statements of the President, Secretary Acheson, or our representatives in the United Nations. It is hard to imagine duller reading.

Yet, it must be admitted that many newspapers, especially the smaller ones, used items from the *Bulletin* because it didn't cost a thing and because, without funds to subscribe to the news service (AP, UP, etc.), it was difficult to find foreign news for their publications. We were able to add considerably to the value of this astronomically expensive project by including a great deal of information about what ECA was doing in Korea. Otherwise it would have been an almost complete loss of time and money, and even at its best it could only reach the small newspaper-reading segment of the population.

The Department of State plans its information program on a global basis. The pattern is as big as all outdoors and is not (despite Washington statements to the contrary) cut to fit any specific area. The last is made entirely in New York and Washington, so that the crucially important matter of policy can be properly controlled. Publications and new films go through a dozen policy meetings and are slashed down to the dead pulp by a dozen red pencils. Generally speaking, the U. S. information centers in Norway, Siam, Iran or Korea receive identical information material. There are only minor differences in the radio product beamed to every corner of the world from Lapland to Capetown. Why should the Icelander think or act in any way differently from his fellow human beings, the Zulu, the Portuguese, or the Mongolian? If he does, he should learn "American" and get over it.

Technically, what comes off the department's assembly line is excellent. But it was not right to show the *UCLA* film in Korea, nor was it right for me to show the picture exhibit of New York's Peter Stuyvesant Village as an example of how to solve a housing problem. These are beautiful films and exhibits and very interesting in their place, but they represent an advanced technology hardly within the dream, much less the practical reach, of a large percentage of the world's population. The Koreans happen to be a polite people and they did not often point this out. The Communists did it for them.

As the months passed and new faces joined us, our operation grew in scope but not in effectiveness. When we were finally going full steam in the Seoul of 1950, just prior to the invasion, our "job layout" was as follows: radio broadcasting and programming, four men (two being engaged in the operation of WVTP); motion pictures, two; libraries, two (the professional librarians had arrived exactly two years after they had been requested); various types of publications including the *Wireless Bulletin* and *American Monthly*, three; cultural relations (musical programs, plays, exchange of students), five; staff of the English Teaching Institute (for which a costly new building had just been constructed when the invasion came), eight; and, to direct all phases of operation in the vast hinterland of Korea (from Seoul), two. The remainder were the secretarial and administrative staff that had also finally arrived.

There was no one in USIS assigned outside the city of Seoul when the invasion came upon us. For months I had done my best to visit the outlying centers, sometimes by Army plane, sometimes by jeep, sometimes by train. When the press of business made visits impossible (I was never assigned a secretary and had to write all reports and correspondence myself), I tried to add the needed personal touch by bringing our Korean managers into Seoul for meetings, briefings, and the review of new films and new programs. Our work was complicated by the fact that even with its two-hundred-man American staff in Korea, Joint Administrative Services could not find time to administer our program, as it was required to by department regulation. We had an enormous appropriation, more than enough to pay our way, but there was a constant struggle to get bills paid, to get supplies to our provincial centers. Korean contractors and businessmen began refusing to bid for our contracts. The embassy's poor credit rating was becoming a byword.

The Korea story would be simplified if we could say categorically that we had failed in everything. Such, however, was not the case. Our work was not all unsuccessful. We undoubtedly influenced men and women here and there. But just as logistics is as important to a propaganda operation as to a military operation, so are proper strategy and, within the strategy, proper tactics. Too often in Korea we used unsuitable weapons and tactics for the terrain and the enemy we faced.

In the months since the North Korean invasion our mili-

tary leaders have discovered a great many things about fighting Communists in Korea. They have discovered that tanks
are useless in certain situations; they have discovered the need
to fight a guerilla warfare, off the highways, in the hills and
forests. In the war to win the hearts and minds of the Koreans
we stayed too much on the highways. By the way we lived
and worked, by the media we emphasized, we often failed to
bring the story of democracy to those willing and able to
learn.

In spite of everything to the contrary, the Department of
State considered its Korean information program a model
operation. The higher officials were flown from Washington
to Seoul to observe and report, the total expenses for these
junkets running in the neighborhood of $10,000. USIS in
Korea was a showcase, but a showcase with one-way glass.
Americans could look in and see a "successful" program
humming with activity; but I fear that the Paks, Kims, and
Lus of South Korea often failed to see what we were doing
for their country. In particular we failed to focus their attention on what the Economic Cooperation Administration was
seeking to do for Korea. ECA was the big American story,
as it has been all over the world, and it was a story we failed
to tell clearly and dramatically.

Chapter 9

The ECA Story

THE very life and stability of the new Korean Republic, its economy, the livelihood of its people, depended upon the $100,000,000 to $150,000,000 of American economic aid appropriated for South Korea and administered by the American Mission to Korea. Korea was like a decapitated human being whose body still sought to function even though separated from head and brain, as a hen is sometimes able to walk for a few moments after the ax has fallen. The 38th Parallel had cut squarely across the economy of the land. The rich mines, the heavy industry, and one-third of the population lay in the North; two-thirds of the population lived in the South, which with the best agricultural land in Korea had become its breadbasket.

The problem of ECA in Korea was therefore to build a new economy to compensate for the lost head; to develop the agricultural lands so that there would be production not only for the South Korean population but also for export. South Korea needed dollars, foreign exchange, so it could buy the raw materials, petroleum products, fertilizer, and consumer goods which it could not produce. Time was important. The life of ECA would be at most two or three years, and South Korea had to be made self-sufficient in that short period. Paralleling the program of economic aid, there also had to be a program of military aid to make the new republic immune to attack from the north.

The economic section of AMIK included some two hundred and fifty American experts in various fields. There were agricultural experts, transportation experts, financial consultants, and engineers and specialists in a dozen fields of industry. The program was directed by Dr. Arthur Bunce, who had spent a number of years in Korea and had a good knowledge of the country, its language, customs, and needs.

ECA had not only a very difficult job to do and a short time in which to do it. There were also problems with the new Korean government and within AMIK itself. The heads of the government knew the importance of ECA aid, indeed could not get what they thought was enough of it. But at the same time Syngman Rhee and his associates were extremely realistic. They had not underestimated the menace from North Korea, and they demanded greater emphasis on military assistance. The two objectives would have been treated as complementary if we had seen the situation in true perspective.

I myself saw the intelligence estimate of North Korean fighting potential sent to Washington in 1950. Our experts reported that the North Korean Army was poorly trained, that it suffered from poor morale, would not receive help from Russia, and could be thrown back by the existing South Korean security forces in case of an attack. I once heard Lt. Col. Vanderpool, an Army intelligence officer assigned to the embassy, say that the South Koreans could not only repel any attack from the north, they could capture Pyongyang, the communist capital, within two weeks if they wished.

Indeed, the fear was expressed from time to time that the South Koreans might attack the North if they became too strong, but Dr. Rhee continued to demand more military aid and to propose large military budgets. ECA, on the basis of intelligence available to it, considered the current military expenditures too high and was continually urging that this part of the budget be reduced for the sake of other projects more in keeping with the industrial revitalization of the country.

However, the troubles of ECA and of our USIS in Korea

did not stem wholly from uncooperative Koreans or from Washington. Some were rooted in AMIK itself. The American Mission was a coordinated mission in name only. It lacked not only coordination but cooperation as well.

The mission was under the direction of three men: Ambassador John Muccio and First Secretaries Harold Noble and James Stewart. Whatever the proposal at hand, the ambassador went into consultation with Stewart and Noble and relied heavily on their judgment. Unhappily, these men had developed an animosity toward Dr. Bunce, the able ECA administrator. In spite of the fact that the staff of Dr. Bunce included economic experts in every possible field the Department of State dispatched a new man to become the embassy's economic counsellor. Thus we had an ECA chief with his vast staff and, superimposed on him, a Foreign Service officer as an added expert on experts, a man holding one of the top grades in the career service.

Dr. Rhee finally became suspicious of this crowd of experts and employed an economic advisor of his own. This was Harold Lady, who had known Rhee during the latter's years of exile in America. With offices in the capitol building, he had easier access to President Rhee than any member of AMIK. Moreover, he had little use for ECA or the embassy proper, and this dislike was reciprocated.

ECA's advice, consequently, did not stand much of a show. The advice Mr. Lady gave President Rhee was often entirely contrary to it, and on the other hand it could also be opposed by the ambassador's personal expert or by Stewart and Noble. No wonder that, to the Koreans, ECA money was often a case of now-you-see-it-now-you-don't. The Communists were busy emphasizing the now-you-don't.

ECA got off to a very bad start in Korea when the Department of State took over American responsibilities. With unbelievable innocence, we made no attempt to supervise and administer the millions of dollars in aid that were poured into the country. The Department of State and the ambassador frowned upon any intervention in Korean affairs (except, of course, to forbid the building of strong security forces). Washington opinion was that we could not interfere in the affairs of a sovereign state, which is theoretically a sound policy; but the inexperience and corruption due to Korean instability could not fail to cause us plenty of headaches. That the dumping of more than $100,000,000 on a struggling economy was in itself "intervention" did not seep into the minds of our policy makers.

During the entire first year of the Korean Republic, Washington received rosy reports of progress from the embassy experts. Meanwhile ECA was sending realistic and honest reports. It was not until a year later, that Washington planners began to see the contradiction in this reporting. Finally, action was taken both by Congress, which voted down an economic aid appropriation for Korea, and by Secretary of State Acheson, who sent a very pointed note to Dr. Rhee. By then so much time had been lost that, though we were totally unaware of what impended, only six months were left to us before the Communists were to strike.

It is interesting to note that while the Department of State refused for a year to allow proper supervision of the aid program, it was quite willing to intervene on another occasion. By mid-1949 the dictatorial ways of President Rhee began to irk some members of the national assembly, and there was a movement to amend the constitution so that cabinet ministers would no longer be responsible to the president. Many educated Koreans felt that this might be a good move, that the original idea of great strength in the executive branch was perhaps a little dangerous and that the Korean people were ready for a new stage in democratic development.

A majority of the assemblymen were apparently for the amendment, until a group of them called on our ambassador for advice. In this instance interference suddenly became American policy! On the advice of the same experts who later were to decry the possibilities of invasion by the North,

Ambassador Muccio advised the assemblymen to drop the amendment project because if the Koreans were so quick to change their new constitution it would indicate to the rest of the world that they did not know their own minds. The greatest criticism of the government was that it could be, and at times was, extremely autocratic. The amendment would have prevented highhandedness; it would have protected the President and his cabinet members from their own inexperience.

The Korean Government, under American tutelage, was forced at last to develop modern budgetary practices,* to balance outgo against income, to tighten up its tax structure. A joint stabilization committee, with members from the cabinet, ECA, and the Military Advisory Group, took control of the nation's economy. The committee, working directly with Koreans, coordinated principal activities, heard experts present every aspect of important questions.

It was not a case of Americans dictating. Often there were arguments; often the Koreans said they just couldn't do this or that. On the whole the Korean Government was impressed with the gravity of the situation, and went to the national assembly with proposals to broaden and implement land reform, raise prices on products and services over which the government had monopolies, and thus bring in new revenues. Politics in Korea does not differ from politics in the United States. It took pressure, courage, and a real desire to act in the national interest, to raise the price of railroad tickets, electric current, coal, and tobacco and to drag some of the greatest business concerns from the control of cabinet members and put them under government corporations.

This is the sort of diplomacy in which the United States has a poor record. It is simple, as *Time* expressed it, to "pant along behind each diplomatic crisis, tossing a handful of money here and a handful there. . . ." But it is extremely dif-

---

* It is interesting to note that Washington planners believe strongly in the principle of the balanced budget. They are also against corruption.

ficult to persuade the leaders of a nation that the money must be used to the greatest benefit of the people as a whole. After all, many of the members of the Korean national assembly were the landlords of Korea. They would be less than human if they had not dragged their feet over this issue. Yet Dr. Bunce and his associates were able to do a very great deal in a short time, and did begin to reach the heart of the problem once they were given the green light.

Any thinking American must realize that economic stability is one of the strongest weapons against communism. Communism breeds rapidly among people who are poorly fed and poorly clothed, and who have no opportunities to achieve better standards. It is especially the possibility of achieving better standards that seems to have the greatest appeal. Communism has an advantage, because its program sounds so simple when compared to the intricacies of ECA with its "counterpart funds," "stabilization boards," "anti-inflation controls," and so on. The communist reform programs are promoted by a fifth column of native leaders who have joined the movement. Consequently, economic aid of the democratic variety must be "sold" by foreigners to a nation's leaders, and they in turn must explain it to the common man.

Some of the ideas our experts advanced met with deep-seated opposition. ECA wanted the Korean people to eat less rice and more barley. Korean rice is of excellent quality and so has a ready export market. From the money that would be received from rice exports, said the experts, the Korean Government could buy needed consumer goods and raw materials in Japan, in the Philippines, or in southeast Asia.

It was part of the program to create a balanced economy. But the Japanese had forced the Koreans to eat barley, and the people's distaste for the measure had not been forgotten. It made the American plan particularly susceptible to communist attack. Was it not prima facie evidence of American imperialism? The Americans were taking the rice of Korea—

the best the farmer could produce—and shipping it out to the hated Japanese, obviously with the double purpose of making money for Americans and of rebuilding Japan. To surmount such misunderstandings requires real diplomacy, a skill we have often lacked.

I have been impressed of late when reading accounts in our American periodicals of the work of Horace Holmes, an American agriculturist in India. His work has interested me particularly, because Holmes was formerly a county agricultural agent in Tennessee. I even met him briefly in my own days of conservation work in the Tennessee Valley. In the Etowah district he had managed to increase wheat production by 50 per cent in a single year. Holmes did a magnificent job in India. He was able to zigzag his way around much opposition, including numerous native superstitions, and put his modern methods to work. So successful has he been that not only is he loved by the Indian people but the Indian Government has asked him to set up two thousand similar experimental units all over India.

Most important from our point of view is the by-product of his success, a heightened friendship for America in a land where we desperately need friendship and understanding. How much better, too, that India's food problem be solved by Indian farmers than by a huge dole financed by the American taxpayer. Horace Holmes has accomplished wonders, not because he is a particularly high-powered expert (his education was not extensive, and his experience was limited to the poor white and colored farmers of western Tennessee), but because he was a student of H. S. Nichols, Tennessee's first pioneer agricultural agent.

When Nichols began his work, the farmers of the South were extremely wary, but Nichols finally persuaded a leading farmer to allow him to prescribe for his worn-out farm. Neighboring farmers came to watch the experiment, to make fun of the "college farmer." As Nichols walked about the farm, he picked up samples of dirt, smelled them, and tossed them aside. He ordered a three-year program of fertilization, rotation, contour farming, all the practices the state university professors were urging. After the second year the farm began to bloom anew, and the extension service was besieged with requests to "send down that young feller who smells the dirt."

Nichols had had very little to work with in the early days. His advice to young Horace Holmes, as it was to the scores of other young agents who studied under him, was "to learn to do by doing with the means at hand: do better when you're able to." Holmes' former colleagues give him the ultimate in tribute when they say, "Horace didn't even have grass roots. He walked in the mud."

There were a few, though not many, among our experts in Korea who were willing to walk in the mud of Korean villages and the filth of the paddy fields. Dr. Bunce himself traveled much in the country, always getting a big smile when he talked the language. Walter Leveau, a fisheries expert, visited every shipyard in the country and stayed in more stinking fishing villages along Korea's intricate coastline, and on more lonely islands, than I can count. He took whatever mode of travel was at hand. Occasionally he went by embassy plane, more often in packed trains, by jeep, or by fishing boat.

Leveau had been a Navy commander, a liaison officer at the famous Higgins boat plants in Louisiana where countless landing craft were built. His great ambition was to rebuild the Korean fishing fleet (Korea had once been sixth in the world in maritime exports). When he couldn't persuade ECA and high Korean Government officials to come and see the canneries, he and the fishermen and cannery people moved a big fisheries exhibit right into the embassy building. It discommoded the noonday poker players by taking their lounge for several days, and even after it was gone an odor of fish hung in the embassy air. Walter was greatly disappointed that he was never able to convert Korean fishermen to the use of American-type lobster traps. There were many large and tender lobsters along the rocky shores, but with the Korean equipment they were caught only by luck.

There were others like Leveau: Mildred Barody in public health, who accomplished marvels in spite of official "no's"; Stan Philippi, former Bureau of Reclamation official; Phil Beck in agriculture. Curiously, one of Beck's important projects was reviving *kudzu*, an oriental forage crop that has been highly successful in our southern states as a green manure to restore nitrogen to the soil. His purpose was to cut down the need for artificial fertilizer (which called for a disproportionate share of the ECA budget), until coal production had been increased, and until fertilizer and electric plants, railroads, etc., had been constructed and were ready for action.

There were also unsung heroes like George Hopkinson, the banking expert whose job it was to make sense out of Korea's chaotic currency situation. George and Helen Hopkinson were among the best of ambassadors, for Helen took it upon herself to enter into the life of the Korean women of Seoul, to become practically a part of their organizations.

Together with the art of giving economic aid and of developing a rapport with the people on a working level, goes the equally important art of convincing the people, official and non-official, that the American-aid dollar is being spent for the good of all. In Korea, the city dweller had a great stake in the agricultural program, which could mean more and better food for his family; the farmer had a stake in the Yongwol power plant and the neighboring coal mines, for these developments could mean better clothing for his family. The stakes, however, remained hidden, because the story of ECA was not put across. The truth is that few Koreans had any conception of what we were trying to do, and they were sorely tempted to listen to the communist version of the American program because it sounded more plausible.

ECA itself had no means of producing or distributing information about its purposes and accomplishments. It necessarily depended entirely upon the United States Information

Service for advertising itself. A coordinated mission would have done that job. But because Jim Stewart (First Secretary, and director of USIS) was incommunicado as far as John Baldridge (ECA's information "staff") was concerned, we failed to get together and work under the same yoke.

Baldridge, a small-town newspaperman from Iowa, had the human touch, an ability to reach the common man, but he was often uninformed of USIS plans and policies, and of its facilities for spreading the much-needed explanation of ECA's role in Korea. At the same time, because staff meetings were thought unnecessary, USIS had only a cursory knowledge of how ECA operated. Yet ECA *was* the American story to Korea, a story which of necessity the Korean people should have known, and which the American taxpayer who footed the bill had every right to think was being told.

A very simple example will explain how ECA operated. Among other things, ECA brought huge amounts of fertilizer to Korea to help increase the food supply. Each sack of fertilizer carried a sticker, stating in both languages that it was "a gift from the people of the United States." But the Korean farmer who received the fertilizer had to pay for it. Having been exploited for generations, the farmer could easily believe the communist story that the United States was in Korea to make money for American business interests. It was never made clear to the people that the money paid for the fertilizer (for all American-aid goods) went into a "counterpart fund" which would eventually be used to rehabilitate factories, build new roads, and develop natural resources. Even an American can be lost in the financial intricacies of such a transaction. To the Korean farmer the "gift" was only one more way of taking cash out of his pocket.

As inflation came into flood tide during the spring of 1950, ECA made a real effort to keep it from running out of control. It put controls on bank loans and tried, successfully, to force up the value of the Korean *won* in relation to the dollar. The immediate result was that many Korean businessmen were ruined through inability to borrow, and because goods they had been selling in Japan and Southeast Asia were increasing in dollar value and decreasing in *won* value. To all appearances it only made matters worse. Some of us could appreciate that ECA was taking the long view, but with the cleavage between that organization and the U. S. Information Service, there was no way by which the long view could be explained to the businessmen. As far as the average Korean tradesman was concerned, he was being put out of business, and ECA was to blame.

ECA is the truest and best response to communist seduction. Properly administered, it disproves the worst the Communists can say about American imperialism. It was well administered in Korea and was helping the economy a great deal, but it was weakened and rendered practically impotent from the point of view of winning friends, because it was never understood by the very people whom it helped. In other words, its psychological impact, which was even more important than its material purpose, was ineffectual. It was as if we were a great industrial concern in which the sales staff had no knowledge of the products being planned or of the potential markets. What, then, would be the point of trying to sell?

The Communists exploited the weakness in ECA. The farmers were told over and over again that Americans were selling their products, their fertilizer, for personal profit. The Pyongyang radio even named our top officials—Muccio, Bunce, and others—as profiting in a particular sale or investment. When the average Korean listened and then looked at the little American empire in Seoul, with its fine homes, its hotels, its cars and taxis, perhaps what the Communists said seemed to make a good deal of sense. No matter how efficiently ECA did its job, no matter how conscientiously Ralph Bricker did his job as "mayor" of our establishment, appearances indicated that the Americans were doing quite well for themselves, thank you.

The President has requested Congress to appropriate $170,-000,000 for the State Department's information program for 1952–1953. This is an increase of 500 per cent during the past five years, an increase justified before Congress by arguing that as America's world-wide commitments increase we must have a more powerful information program to explain just what we are doing. The State Department information staff already totals over ten thousand men and women (more than the combined staffs of the Associated Press, the National Broadcasting Company, and Metro-Goldwyn-Mayer), and the new appropriation, if approved, will doubtless add hundreds or perhaps thousands more.

I wonder how well we can tell the story if we continue to operate as we did in Korea where the much-vaunted coordination was lacking, where not one of a staff of thirty-four Americans engaged in the information program was stationed outside the city of Seoul. How well will Hollywood-type movies, English teaching institutes, English-language libraries, do the job? It certainly is not an easy job, with the barriers of language, customs, and superstitions and with the constant competition of the communist story. Still, men like Holmes, Leveau, and Baldridge have proved that the American technician or expert can, if willing, reach the person he is sent to help.

Perhaps the experiences of AMIK in Korea, and of Horace Holmes in India, also point up the need for less ambitious and more practical approaches to the problems. Perhaps instead of mutual assistance programs costing millions and embracing every phase of a nation's economic life, we need instead a few small "pilot" projects. I can easily visualize what could be done in one Korean *gun* (county). Take the Taechun Beach area, with its agricultural, forestry, and fisheries possibilities; and think what might be accomplished by a group of perhaps five able and conscientious Americans and their wives if they lived there and worked out with the local Korean officials a simple program to solve the economic problems of that community. If they were the right people and used the right approach, officials of other counties would take note in time, would begin to imitate, to follow suit.

Such projects are far from visionary. They can be accomplished without vast expenditures of U. S. Government funds. Already one church in Oklahoma, seeing the possibilities, has organized what it calls World Assistance, Inc., and has dispatched its own experts to India. Think what the Ford Foundation might do with such a practical and *inexpensive* approach—is already attempting to do to a limited extent.

Chapter 10

Puppets and Marionettes

THERE were times when we approached the magic formula, days when it seemed we had found the key to solve the riddle of international misconceptions, misunderstandings, dislike, even hate. I remember in particular a morning in May 1948, when we were campaigning for free elections in the mountains of Kangwon Province.

We had driven our heavily loaded jeep and trailer into a tiny amphitheatre close to a little village which, in turn, was close to the deadly Parallel. We had, after considerable map reading and scouting by jeep, chosen the spot for an important showing of our propaganda film, *The People Vote*. Both the UN Commission and Military Government were anxious to make a good showing along the border, where communist opposition to the proposed election was expected to be feverish, perhaps even violent. We had left Peacock Mountain and gone north into the hills, in spite of warnings from Seoul that the mountainous areas of Kangwon were impassable; and we had found an ideal location for setting up shop.

True, this corner of South Korea is extremely rugged, as men of our Third Army Division and First Marines have learned. Its village squares are almost as vertical as they are horizontal. The pines that blanket the mountains sweep down to the rivers and are tucked tightly along steep banks. But here and there are bowl-shaped clearings laid out in rice paddies. The paddies are still bone dry in early May, and one of them made a perfect amphitheatre for a film showing. The audience squatted on the rising levels, and we set the projector opposite on the wall of a dike. For two hours before sundown our jeep had thundered up and down the narrow valleys and deep ravines of the area, announcing the big show, and by dark the people were slowly filling the "house." They came in family groups, the master walking ahead, the women and children following behind at a respectful distance. The women carried babies strapped on their backs.

As dark settled down, with the only light coming from our headlights and projection apparatus, the scene was a strange and beautiful one. The white gowns of some five thousand Koreans were a soft snowfall along the paddies and dikes, extending upward into the blackness of the pine woods. I can hear, as if it were yesterday, the drone of the portable generator in the background, the shuffling of restless feet on the dry earth, the chatter of children massed close under the screen. I can hear Elsie's voice as she went before the mike for words of explanation in a tongue and in terms the people knew. How well we had learned even by then, that the mere presence of a Korean-speaking American, and especially an American woman, melted the reserves of these shy people and developed a quick intimacy.

After half an hour of recorded music, played while the audience gathered and settled down, we were ready to start. The district political leader was scheduled to make a short introductory speech. We had specifically emphasized the shortness when we had called upon him, knowing as we did that Koreans are natural-born orators, but we were only partially successful in stemming the tide. When it was over, Elsie gave a further explanation of the coming elections (Hong Shin and Pak were absent with other teams), urging everyone to vote as he wished, for the candidate of his choice. Her perfect handling of the language brought forth exclamations of surprise and approval from the audience: "Ai-go," and "Chota."

During the next hour these people saw a simple motion

picture. It had been filmed in Korea; it was in the Korean language; it used well-known Korean actors. The story had an election—*the* election—as its motif. The hero was a candidate for office. He was straightforward and honest in the promises he made. The villain was a candidate for the same office. He promised everything, meant none of it, but had the support of some strong-arm men. There was a scene in which the question of women voting was discussed. The drama closed on a scene in which everyone, even an old man who was at first uninterested, turned out on election day, and of course the hero won. As a grand finale, the hero delivered his maiden speech in the national assembly, a stirring speech on a democratic theme.

Moving about in the darkness, checking ground wires, finding places for the late comers, I felt a thrill of satisfaction and pride. Everywhere, I heard exclamations of appreciation, laughter, sighs, squeals of delight. The audience was living the story, tense and interested. This was propaganda at its best. We had reached our objective with something that could be comprehended. And it paid off. Some five hundred North Koreans had slipped across the Parallel that night to see the picture. And 97 per cent of the district voted on May 10.

That night in the paddy fields we had all the ingredients of a successful propaganda program, ingredients that can be used just as successfully to tell the story of ECA, Point Four, military assistance. Our message could be understood, and it was taken to the people where they lived. The film produced with equipment so ramshackle some of it had to be held together with baling wire, was made in three weeks, at a cost of perhaps $4,000. It was presented by an American speaking the language and knowing the people and the customs. Our equipment was simple: a rickety jeep, a jeep trailer, a portable generator and a screen made from a few yards of cheap Korean muslin. The cost of a similar film made in Washington by the Department of State would run into tens of thousands and be months, even years, in the process.

We often chafed under the Army's regimentation and indifference, but we were to realize later that the Army applied a far more direct, simple, and effective strategy in its approach to a given problem than AMIK. It was not necessary for our ideas to be checked pro and con by panel after panel of "experts," for every project to be screened by a series of policy meetings before action was taken. If this had been so, we obviously could never have produced a feature film in a matter of weeks.

The Army also allowed a considerable degree of local autonomy for tactical procedure. We could produce posters, motion pictures, exhibits, and radio programs, on our own. We had little practical help from Washington, before or after we became an adjunct of the Department of State. All our effective propaganda weapons, before or after, were forged in Korea. Army equipment was often poor, the product of our efforts often mediocre from a technical standpoint, but the authority to act made it possible for us to move quickly and to the point. Not only did we have the election film, in as many copies as we needed, but we were supplied the mobile equipment (such as it was) to rush the film to the public. In no time flat, our Chunchon staff had travelled five thousand miles, shown the film to several hundred thousand people, and had distributed voting information and directions to the most remote mountain communities. I shudder to think how impossible this would have been if we had had to go through the channels of the Department of State.

Charles Tanner was the young American genius in charge of film production in our Office of Civil Information under Army. He produced many other titles in addition to *The People Vote*. Some were merely newsreels, others were made for specific situations. Now and again, the sound tracks were fuzzy; occasionally the script was poor. But the pictures helped fill a very great need, cost very little, and were, I believe, the best propaganda films I have ever seen.

Tanner stayed on with us when the Department of State took over. At first the department was extremely skeptical

of the whole idea of local production. We were able, however, to show the team of experts that descended on Korea
after my Washington trip the need for continued local production, provided we agreed to a certain amount of script
approval in advance. Had we had true coordination, real
team work, and men in the provinces to supervise the results,
we could have told the ECA story in effective terms. Washington, however, always seemed to view this upstart film
production with a rather jaundiced eye, preferring to have
the bulk of our material planned, written, and produced in
the States.

Present investigation of the department gives me hope that
there has been a change of viewpoint. At least, Tanner is still
employed by the department and has been sent to Manila
where a regional production center has been established. The
word *regional* implies that films and other materials are to
be produced in Manila for all the Far East. How Manila can
furnish the proper backgrounds and actors for pictures to be
shown on Formosa or in Indochina and Thailand, I do not
know. At least the department has moved in the right direction, and perhaps there is hope of eventually reaching various
Asiatic peoples with a story that can be understood and put
to work practically and spiritually for our side.

After my return from the Far East, I was employed briefly
as a consultant by the Department of the Army, and my first
task was to review motion pictures the Army was making
for use in Japan and in areas of Korea retaken from the Communists. The Army information program is the responsibility of the Reorientation Branch, a small unit tucked away in
downtown New York. There a staff of perhaps half a dozen
men and women plan, write, and direct the production of
propaganda films. I was very agreeably impressed by the
simplicity and efficiency of this operation.

Most of the pictures present everyday phases of American
life that parallel the lives of people in unindustrialized areas.
Each film deals succinctly with a strictly limited subject: the
office worker, the farmer, life in a small town. Production

of a film may take as little as six or eight weeks. The average cost is perhaps a tenth that of a State Department film. Army's film division does attempt to cooperate with the Department of State's Division of International Motion Pictures, but without much success. Its productions are not considered professional. I have wondered whether the success achieved in the democratization of Japan is not due, in large part, to the fact the Army supervised the Information Service there. Unfortunately, it will not do so when the peace treaty becomes fully effective.

To get back to Seoul. Miss Berta Metzger was one among the hundreds of women working in Occupation and Military Government offices in 1948 and 1949. It was a hobby of hers that opened another door for us in our attempt to go straight to the Korean mind. Miss Metzger had traveled throughout Asia collecting native legends to use in puppet shows. She had produced shows in half a dozen countries and came to us in the Office of Civil Information with the purpose of doing similar work in Korea. I must admit that I, for one, was skeptical. I invited Miss Metzger and her puppet troupe to the shrine for a trial performance or two. The plays she put on for us were built entirely around Korean legends and folk tales, with little ideological implication of any kind. The result was startling. This was not entertainment merely for children, or the illiterate; the puppets obviously appealed to people in every walk of life.

Miss Metzger left Korea when the Occupation ended, but by dint of loud argument I was able to retrieve her venture from death when the State Department took over. I began to write the scripts for the shows we presented, and Elsie, with a group of Korean "actors," made the puppets and the costumes, pulled the strings, and were the voices. A talented young Korean, Cooper Kim (he had chosen Gary Cooper's last name as his first, Cooper being an actor and the name being easily pronounced in Korean), was our star performer and chief of our puppet section.

As a way of spreading anticommunist propaganda or tell-

ing the ECA story, the puppet shows worked like a charm.
Our first production, my first venture as a playwright, was
a thriller, a modern masterpiece called *Temptation*. Cooper
Kim immediately revised it beyond all recognition! Its hero
was a young South Korean soldier who fell in love with a
beautiful *kisang* (dancing girl) who was, of course, the
communist spy from North Korea. But all was well that
ended well. A few bad people got killed while he was making up his mind, but the young soldier finally saw the error
of his ways and gave up the girl for the sake of his country.
It was a very simple story indeed, but it presented one of the
burning issues of the day in Korea. This one play had packed
into it more sensible and pertinent anticommunist propaganda than all the films the Department of State has ever
produced.

No matter how our stories developed, the villains were
usually Communists, always anti-democrats; the heroes were
patriots equally passionate in their espousal of democracy.
The plays were rich in humor, poking constant fun at Kim
Il Sung, Stalin, and Mao Tse-tung. Falling back on Korean
legends for source material that would be easily recognized,
we often used animals to explain an idea—the *Animal Farm*
technique. In one play, for instance, the greedy profiteer,
who was doing his level best to spoil the good effects of
ECA, appeared in the guise of the sly old fox, an animal
loathed and feared by the countryfolk of Korea. The tiger,
the peacock, the fox—all have special connotations for Koreans. It was no great feat to weave these animals into a story
in such a way that the point was easily and quickly put
across. No confusing Washington dialect was included.

We had to scrounge for material to make costumes and
sets. I was amazed when I wandered into our auditorium in
Seoul one day to find a new play in rehearsal with the puppets decked out in parts of my hunting clothes. And it was
also difficult to persuade the embassy to afford us transportation into the country.

The matter of employing puppeteers created quite a crisis. Although on the American and Korean staffs we had such undiplomatic posts as menu planner and liquor-store operator, the State Department manual just did not include a job description to fit a puppeteer. We wound up by listing our actors as housekeepers (several grades of these are provided for—housekeeping is obviously an important diplomatic job). Cooper Kim was classified as a technician, grade eleven.

Not long ago, I saw one of the State Department's new films for overseas. I am told it was two years in production and cost $120,000. I was eaten alive with jealousy for what a fraction of this sum might have accomplished if properly spent in the mountains and rice paddies of Korea. The average cost of one of our plays (costumes, salaries while in rehearsal, sets) ranged from $50 to $75, and Cooper Kim's salary was 22,000 *won* a month (the equivalent of $10).

Puppet shows, in addition to being inexpensive, can easily be written around the legends common to every country in the world. The story tells itself through the gyrations of the puppets; it needs no American interpreter. The only problem is to provide transportation for the crew of four or five actors who must pull the strings and provide the voices of the characters. At times in Korea, when we could not get a truck, our puppeteers went out by train. From time to time the Korean sponsoring organizations were so anxious to bill our performance that transportation was provided.

In spite of the effectiveness of our shows, it was very difficult to create interest in them at home. I sent Washington a complete picture story of the operation, showing our puppets in action, the crowds, the behind-the-scenes excitement. Several months later when I returned briefly to the States, I found, to my surprise, that the pictures had never been circulated or used in any way. The key to this lack of interest can be found in the words of the official who told me frankly that the State Department could hardly go before Congress and ask money for puppets! After all, the complete cost of a show, including salaries for the length of the run, was only $75. That was not money. Some Broadway production, transported *in toto* to Seoul, might impress Congress. As for me, I was merely interested in trying to impress the people of Korea.

I heard the same argument recently when, as an Army consultant in New York, I tried hard to sell the idea of puppet shows, thinking that Cooper Kim and his associates might still be alive and could be rounded up to begin again. I even foresaw movies being made of our original shows so that thousands more could be reached throughout Korea; perhaps the films could even be smuggled into North Korea. The budget-conscious, Congress-conscious colonel in charge was interested but said that what a congressional committee would do to a budget listing puppet shows, costumes, and actors was more than he dared to contemplate. Many of us, including members of the Congress, have become so mesmerized by the efficiency of such media as radio and television that we tend to forget there are parts of the world where much simpler and less expensive methods will do the job, and do it better.

I became very much interested in extending our movie and puppet work into the hundreds of islands that lie off the western coast of Korea. As far back as 1948, Hong Shin had told me that the Communists would try to use these islands as bases for subversive activities and eventually military attack. We already had before us the example of Cheju Island off the southwest coast, which had been a festering sore of communist intrigue and pillage for three years.

I determined to buy a boat and develop a floating mobile unit. I spent many hours in the harbor of Inchon, looking over the boats for sale. None of them were bargains. David Ahn, Korean manager of our information center at Inchon, was equally interested in the project. He finally located a nameless diesel-powered craft of indeterminate age and ownership. I asked an AMIK engineer to check the engines, and we made some trial runs into the outer harbor. The boat was obviously no great shakes, but it appeared to be all we needed to cross the short stretches of quiet water to the islands.

Now, though money was found in the budget for the ship's purchase and overhaul, we suddenly found ourselves faced with another obstacle. According to law, the Department of State cannot purchase motor vehicles without specific congressional approval. Was our boat classified as a motor vehicle? Cables flashed back and forth. The final decision from Washington was that it was not so classified, and payment was made.

As soon as the final papers were signed, Ahn explained that according to Korean maritime regulations the boat had to be christened and registered. He and his friends had decided upon a name which was awaiting my approval: *S. S. Judge Medina!* The trial of the twelve top Communists in America had just been concluded, and David was much impressed with Judge Harold Medina's charge to the jury (Korean newspapers had carried many stories of the trial). David Ahn felt that it would be particularly appropriate to christen our craft the *Medina*, in the hope it would, like the judge, help to obstruct the forces of communism.

Unfortunately, I resigned from the embassy staff soon after the *Judge* was readied for duty, and an embassy expert, getting wind of our plans, instituted another inspection. In spite of the fact that the boat was only intended to cruise among the sheltered inside passages, it was declared unseaworthy. But since it had been bought and paid for, some use had to be found for the ship. Although she finally ended up in a blaze of glory during the invasion, the use the embassy found for the *S. S. Judge Medina* (also known as "Caldwell's folly") was to cruise among the lovely islands of Inchon harbor with embassy picnic and swimming parties. She was seaworthy enough for that.

Chapter 11

Diplomat to Fishmonger

BY THE END of 1949 the sands had begun to run out as far as my career in the Department of State was concerned. For many months I had argued against the manner in which we operated, the methods used in handling our funds, the lack of proper administrative support from JAS. Finally I had written personal letters to a couple of friends in the department in Washington, asking about the possibilities of reassignment.

This simple action on my part was a violation of an unwritten law of the Foreign Service. One does not (unless one knows the right man in the right place of power) write personal letters; one does not ask for reassignment; one does not criticize, even in a personal and friendly manner. Or as W. Walton Butterworth (former counsellor of Embassy with rank of Minister, in Nanking, and later Assistant Secretary for Far Eastern Affairs under Marshall) once said to me: "In the Foreign Service one does not express, or have, opinions about anything."

The answer to my exploratory letters regarding reassignment was a curt telegram from Washington transferring me from Seoul to Washington at once. After one has worked in the department a number of years, it is a simple matter to read between the lines of telegrams and letters. Certain phrases mean certain things. The curtness, the urgency, of the telegram could only mean that there was trouble brewing for me.

After all, even though in seven years of service I consistently received excellent efficiency ratings and had been sin-gled out time and again for praise and commendation, my record was fundamentally bad. The anticommunist report I had written in 1946, and the displeasure it had brought upon me from Mr. Butterworth and General Marshall, were a blot on my record that could not be erased. Mr. Butterworth had thought so poorly of me that he had done an unusual thing: he had sent to Washington a personal denunciation. Later I was allowed to read this message in Washington and was deeply impressed by the adjectives used in describing me. The one that has stayed with me longest is "heinous." In the dictionary I found it meant "hateful; hatefully bad; odious; atrocious, giving great offense."

The public does not generally realize that most Foreign Service officers (non-career) can be dismissed at any time, without recourse to a hearing, without any formal preferring of charges. It is only the career officers (of whom there were perhaps twenty among our hundreds in AMIK) who have any protection. They can be denounced publicly, can even be found to be a security risk by the FBI, and yet stay on forever.

The Foreign Service does have subtle ways of punishing career officers who get out of line, who perhaps receive too much publicity. An officer who distinguished himself by saving the Chinese staff of the embassy during the rape of Nanking in 1937 (while his superiors took to their heels) was punished for years by receiving no further promotion and by assignments to out-of-the-way spots. Career officer Angus Ward, whom the Communists in Manchuria arrested, tried, and held for months, has been assigned to the heart of Africa, presumably because of the very great publicity at-tending his release. The rank-and-file staff or reserve officer does not receive even these reprieves.

My heart was in Korea. I wanted to stay on and watch the development of the country and the people. I did not know what, if any, charges awaited me in Washington. Indeed, by now a miasma of doubt has settled over my "case," and I shall possibly never know. Remembering Mr. Butterworth's tender epithets, I thought it probable that unpleasantness was in store. I simply resigned.

Elsie had already indicated her own desire to resign at the end of December 1949. Since the loss of both of us at the same time would cripple the operation, she agreed, at the request of the ambassador, to stay on until a replacement arrived. The ambassador also asked me to continue for several months. This I agreed to do, but when the department heard of the plan, another telegram arrived. It said, in effect, that my presence, even until a replacement arrived, was unthinkable. I was happy to be out, to be away from the sixteen-hour-a-day grind and the nerve-wracking frustrations. But the department's action did hurt me. The cables and correspondence between the embassy and Washington were not classified, which meant they were read by dozens of American and Korean clerks and officers. I was forced to leave under a cloud and, as far as my fellow workers were concerned, could have committed almost any crime short of murder.

On February 1, 1950, Elsie and I moved from our embassy home on Seoul's "Gold Coast" into a rented house in the Severance Hospital compound. By resigning, I automatically deprived myself of the protectives of the American Mission in Korea. Since Elsie was, at embassy request, still working, I could have argued the point. AMIK was supporting mothers-in-law, fathers-in-law and various other in-laws. But in a way I felt it would help me more if I cut off completely. The government-owned-and-furnished houses, the servants, free fuel, and free electricity slowly conspire to destroy one's independence, to make one a creature of government.

We took with us the servants we had—old Shin-se-bang, the cook; Skeezix, the houseboy; and little Ok-chin, the house-and-laundry girl. However, living in AMIK luxury had become a matter of importance to face-conscious young Koreans. When Skeezix realized that the Caldwells had figuratively moved across the tracks, he resigned, even though we were paying for his education as well as his salary.

I was allowed to keep a "Washington" (embassy) phone, since we lived in the hospital compound and the phone might be useful for emergency medical service. Little did we know, at the time, how important the phone was to be, waking us one dark night five months later in time to join the other American refugees. And as long as Elsie was employed we had privileges at the super market, and she retained her PX card. Otherwise, I was outside, with the Koreans and the missionaries. The latter had lost, under AMIK, the privileges they had been granted under Army Occupation.

Yet even such living was a luxury for us. We had been born and brought up in missionary families in China and Korea, and we had known varying degrees of hardship and poverty. Having always done in Rome more or less what the Romans did, we found it comparatively easy to do so again. Indeed, we found it less embarrassing and more satisfying, if we more nearly shared the Korean way of life instead of trying to implant an American substitute. We soon found ourselves living more and more off the land, using the super market less and less. We discovered butchers who sold fresh and fairly tender chunks of beef. The cut was never recognizable, but with plenty of cooking it was palatable. In the Korean fish markets we found excellent fresh fish, prawns, and oysters.

It was an excursion into the big fish market in Seoul that gave me a notion. I had been casting about for a way to bring in a little cash while I was developing a pottery business I planned to open in Kaesong. I can safely say that I am the only ex-diplomat who made his living, even for a short period, by selling fish. From reserve officer of the Foreign Service, attaché of a United States Embassy, to fishmonger!

I conceived the idea of supplying the embassy hotels and the super market with guaranteed fresh sea food. The fish

the Americans served was cold-storage, some of it having
been on ice for as long as two years. Meat was of like vintage.
Ralph Bricker agreed to let me sell fresh-caught fish and
shrimps to the embassy. It was quite an undertaking, since
the best came from Pusan, nearly three hundred miles away.
I hired a young Korean helper who had an uncle with a fish
market in Pusan. Suh E Ton (who has since come to America
as a Department of State exchange student) went to Pusan,
took the fish right off the boats, packed them in ice, and per-
sonally brought them to Seoul by slow freight.

To the horrified amazement of Koreans and Americans
alike, I met the fish in the Seoul freight yards and transported
them to the super market and the hotels in my car. I naturally lost a great deal of face in certain circles. For weeks I
had to ignore the giggles among the embassy girls when I
passed, and the raucous shouts of "Fish!" when I entered
the embassy.

It wasn't for long. Before many weeks I was launched in
my pottery business. During a trip to our information center
at Kaesong, months before, I had visited a tiny pottery plant
on the outskirts of the city and had there discovered some of
the most exquisite ceramic work I had ever seen in the Orient. I made friends with the owner, Mr. Hwang, and he told
me his story.

During the Koryo Dynasty (918–1392 A.D.) Kaesong had
been Korea's capital. It was a period when the country's cultural development was at its peak. The artisans of China and
Japan came from afar to study and copy the beautiful glazes
and designs of Koryo porcelain, known throughout the Orient as celadon. The art reached its zenith in the thirteenth
and fourteenth centuries and then went into a decline. The
Koryo kings had been overthrown, and the new Li Dynasty,
which was in power until the Japanese seized Korea, produced hardly any truly indigenous art.

Only in tiny, forgotten pockets, such as the Kaesong pottery plant, were the ancient ceramic patterns and methods

being kept alive. The pottery was being made in very small quantities, to be sure, but it was an almost perfect reproduction of Koryo designs. Mr. Hwang claimed that his family had passed down the secret of the glazes from generation to generation for nearly four hundred years.

It seemed to me that here was an opportunity to do something worth-while for myself and possibly helpful to the Korean economy. The Koreans had, in other years, made many beautiful things. Kaesong had once been the furniture-making capital of the country, and brass-bound chests, two and three hundred years old, could still be found in the city. I saw many other handicraft possibilities: work in brass, mother-of-pearl, linen. Korean women could be engaged to weave and embroider in their homes.

In other words, there appeared to be a potentially very large handicraft industry in Korea. It could eventually bring in millions of badly needed export dollars and provide a livelihood for hundreds of people in small towns and villages. When I recalled what Japan had done the world over in selling its toys, souvenirs, and art works, I began to have grandiose illusions!

Through Mr. Suh E Ton, now advanced to the position of chief clerk from that of procurer of fish, I began to negotiate with Mr. Hwang. I wanted to work out a partnership in which I would help to finance the expansion of the little plant. I would help in developing new designs to be used in making dinner, tea, and coffee sets of the beautiful old celadon for popular export. At the same time, I set out to scour the country for other handicraft products which might go in America. It was wonderfully refreshing work, but slow, as all business in the Orient must be.

Mr. Hwang was very suspicious of my ideas at first. He had tried working with another American during the Occupation and had found himself making thick white coffee mugs for a Military Government mess. He had no conception of the problems of merchandising, of getting goods through American customs, of the necessity of excellent and uniform quality. Some of the articles he most loved to make I knew would have no sale among Americans. Mr. Hwang had also heard the communist song of American imperialism, selfishness, and corruption and for a time was having none of me. I made innumerable trips north across the Imjin River into towns like Panmunjun, which were, months later, to become so much a part of our thoughts and lives in the United States. I entertained Mr. Hwang in Kaesong and in Seoul. I asked the help and intervention, in oriental style, of mutual Korean friends.

I moved slowly; and my patience was sorely taxed at times, for at the moment when I thought an understanding had been reached, Mr. Hwang would shy off. Victory finally came, after a sixth trip to Kaesong. I had left Mr. Suh behind to try to clinch the deal with Mr. Hwang. Two days later a letter came from Mr. Suh, a letter which was unconsciously rich in some of the business complications of the Orient: "Had a lot of chat with Mr. Hwang last night at the restaurant. While he as well as me was drunk we talked frankly and his idea was that he is not after money from beginning to end. There got to be something spiritual other than money to get our diplomacy 100 per cent effective.

"Anyway he said you are an American who understand Korean situation better than any others whom he has met so far. In Mr. Hwang's case my opinion is to wait with utmost patience. About five other foreign traders are after him and he is holding them all calmly watching how you would behave if sometimes he cannot keep promise for unavoidable reasons. . . . My conclusion about concerning Mr. Hwang is that he is a reliable young man and if we stick to him with patience plus our spiritual tolerance it would not be impossible to handle him."

Shortly thereafter, Mr. Hwang decided I was spiritual enough and we signed a contract. I found myself part owner, sales manager, advertising manager, and director of design, of a Korean pottery plant which lay just three hundred yards from North Korean positions on the Parallel. These positions bristled with guns, and occasionally the North Koreans dropped a few mortar shells into the city, just to keep us in mind of their presence. In the light of what was to happen, the Kaesong pottery venture was undoubtedly foolish on my part; but I had read our official American intelligence reports and believed the supposition that the North Koreans would not and could not attack, that the only problem was an occasional practice shot just to upset the South Koreans' nerves.

I did not put all my eggs in Mr. Hwang's basket. Mr. Suh continued to scour the country for me. In the far south, in the Cholla provinces, we located some beautiful bamboo work—baskets, window shades and screens—and we put a dozen women to work making exquisite table settings from Korean "mourning cloth." A number of Americans in AMIK became very much interested in what I was doing and gave me new ideas. I heard for instance that hand-painted silk scarfs were all the rage in America. Through Slim Kim, in the USIS art section, we located an excellent artist and soon added genuine hand painted scarfs to our export trade.

A buyer for a large art shop on the west coast of America arrived and actually ordered some of my pottery. In the meantime, as Mr. Hwang and I experimented with new designs for coffee and tea sets, we were able to sell on the Korean market. A steady stream from AMIK came to our house in the Severance compound to look at the pottery, the brass-bound chests, and the table mats, and most of them went away with a purchase.

Until he left for America to study at the University of Michigan, Mr. Suh remained my loyal right-hand man. He handled all my money, all my contacts with my Korean producers, and continued as a sort of talent scout. Mr. Suh's only problem was that he couldn't resist a bargain and his idea of a bargain could easily be something I had a hard time selling.

He came back from one trip with a very poorly prepared leopard-skin rug. After all, it had been a real bargain—only 40,000 Korean *won!*

My life as an entrepreneur lasted no more than five months, but during that period I had an opportunity to see AMIK and our whole Korean operation almost through Korean eyes, for many of my problems were those of Korean businessmen. From American high officialdom I received no encouragement whatsoever in the opportunities I was bringing to light. It was more exciting to build new factories and new railroads. The fact that an industry complementing the Korean way of life was there for the developing, was something they could not grasp. My pottery, my chests, my decorative articles, didn't impress them, in spite of the fact that I was beginning to get orders from Americans in Japan and even from the United States.

However, some of the ECA men of lesser rank eventually became much interested in the possibilities. The ECA industries division decided that handicrafts was worth a try, and that a survey should be made of products and sales possibilities in the States. I was thrilled at the idea. I asked permission to bid on making such a survey and was told I might. Mr. Suh and I carefully worked out a plan and estimated the expenses involved, adding a reasonable amount for our time and effort. Since I was in on the ground floor, so to speak, had already done much of the work, had uncovered possible money-makers in every province, and had even made sales contacts in America, I was able to make a reasonable estimate: $1,200 for two months' work. Perhaps it is an indication of our times that my little bid was rejected in favor of one made by a New York antique and curio dealer who had never been in Korea. He agreed to do the job in two years for $60,000.

The more I entered the problems of making a living in Korea, the more I realized the necessity of seeing that ECA was understood by the Koreans, especially by the businessmen. The red tape that had all but hamstrung foreign trade was incomprehensible even to me. If I operated on the ECA-enforced exchange rate, it would be impossible for me to sell anything anywhere. According to ECA-approved laws, I couldn't keep any profit in dollars, provided I was lucky enough to make a profit. While on the one hand encouraging foreign trade, and also supposedly encouraging American businessmen, ECA on the other hand made it almost impossible to do any business. The regulations were set up to control inflation, but a by-product was a stifling of trade.

Through the help of some ECA friends and the sympathy of the Koreans, I gradually found ways to stay just within the maze of laws and regulations. I had saved a little money (in dollars, of course), enough, I thought, to carry me until I was in real production. But I couldn't pay Mr. Hwang or my other producers in dollars. I had to have *won*. Since I would go out of business if I bought my *won* at the official rate, I was forced to make some strange deals. Once I sold my "advisory services" as an "American economic expert" to a Korean businessman who was authorized to receive dollars, since he was in foreign trade. The rate he paid was the black-market rate. No one with legitimate dollars would sell to him at the legal rate. He needed dollars; I needed *won*. I found someone else who had relatives in America. The relatives needed dollars. He was willing to sell me *won* at a good rate. No transaction violated the letter of the law though its spirit took a beating. We just avoided mention of exchange rates and traded dollars for *won*.

I found that it would be impossible to export anything in my own name. The American Government seems to have slight interest in helping the small businessman abroad. If I used my own name, I couldn't keep a dollar I made. I would have millions of *won*, no doubt, but my insurance company in America was unlikely to accept *won* as payment for my insurance premiums. There were few other American businessmen in Korea, and I could see why! Those who had come used every ingenious dodge invented by man. One had an unwritten understanding with an American buyer that the price quoted on a given product was actually 20 per cent less than should have been asked. That extra 20 per cent never showed up in invoices and was automatically deposited in an American bank to the credit of the exporter in Korea. In this way, some Koreans were able to build up cozy dollar deposits in America.

I decided not to operate in this manner. Through Jack Thorne, ECA's foreign trade consultant, I was introduced to a Mr. Liu who had both *won* and dollars. He appreciated the need for American "know-how." In return for allowing me to handle selling, designing, etc., with Mr. Hwang, he would pay me a percentage of profits in dollars as an "advisor" to his tungsten importing business. He and his partners would supply the *won* needed for our operations in Korea. It sounds complicated, and it was.

Agreement with Mr. Liu was reached just before the lid blew off in Korea, and the plan was never carried out. In the meanwhile, I had struggled along as best I could. I had made very little money but was building faith and respect among my Korean employees and manufacturers. I myself was learning a way of life for which my college education had never prepared me.

My business life gave me far more leisure than I had had in two years. On week ends, Elsie and I drove to Taechun Beach to spend a day or so in our Korean cottage. On good highways in America, a drive of 135 miles requires less than three hours. In Korea it took six to eight hours to cover the same distance—with no flats! It was worth it. There was good hunting all along the way. More and more often friends came with us, sometimes for the hunting, sometimes for the beach only.

The house had paper doors and windows and couldn't be locked. When we first built it, we were warned that the residents of the fishing village just over the hill would clean us out of everything we left there. We solved this problem oriental style: we hired as caretaker one of the leading thieves in the village. It became a point of honor with him to see that our house was well taken care of. We never lost a thing.

My changed way of life did more than give me time in the country. In Seoul, as in most of the Far East, there is a sharp cleavage between the two American communities, the official and the missionary. Our trips to the beach and our residence in the Severance Hospital compound (the hospital was operated jointly by three denominations) inevitably drew us more and more into the missionary circles of Korea. Although I am the son of a missionary, I had never been particularly interested in missionary work, having nothing more than a deep-seated family loyalty for the work of my fathers. But as I moved first into the no man's land between AMIK and the missionaries, then more and more into the missionary bailiwick, I inevitably began to make comparisons.

AMIK, as a fledgling government enterprise, was spending millions of dollars to build a modern superstructure on a strange and ancient base. With few exceptions, it worked in isolation from the Koreans in the paddy fields and the mountain villages. It worked through bureaus and agencies, through sections and subsections, churning over the endless reams of directives, reports, and carbons of government forms. It was staffed by hundreds of high-salaried men and women who lived in relative luxury, and perhaps tended to think accordingly, in a land of poverty.

The missionary enterprise, on the other hand, flowed into the base of Korean life. It had colleges and medical institutions, and its churches stood in every Korean town or city. The missionary establishment was largely self-supporting. Its men and women had been in Korea for many years, and they travelled the roads and trails into the remotest villages of the country. They trained Koreans to administer the hospitals and colleges. To them, Korea was not a page for the files but human life. Their objective was the personal encounter.

I began to wonder whether the AMIK official and the missionary, the administrative and the personal, could not complement each other in some very tangible manner. At least, the missionaries and their work are necessary to our understanding of the Korea story.

Chapter 12

The Missionary Story

IN THE years immediately after the end of World War II much of the Far East was war-ravaged. The United States Army ran Japan, Korea, and Okinawa and was present in such numbers in the Philippines, parts of China, and Formosa that the local way of life was almost the U. S. Army way of life. The Army (or the Navy) controlled shipping and transportation; Army post offices functioned for months and even years while native postal systems were being rehabilitated. The Army PX, the commissary, Army-marked jeeps, all became a part of the Orient. Americans used military script as currency throughout much of the Orient. This was true in Korea until the communist invasion even though Korea had been an independent nation for nearly two years.

Economic conditions being as they were, all Americans were dependent upon the Army for logistic support, and this included the missionaries. For instance, no missionary could return to Korea or Japan without Army permission. His trip back was made on an Army transport, and when he arrived in Korea he had practically the status of a civilian employee of the army. But the missionaries were grateful for such status and often reciprocated by providing the Army with missionary housing. The life of missionaries in postwar Korea would have been difficult indeed without the PX, the APO, and the commissary.

Fundamentally, economic conditions had not changed greatly when the State Department took over in Korea. Transportation to America (except for the air service provided by Northwest Airlines) was still largely U. S. Government controlled. Except for British shipping from Hong Kong and communist China, practically no "free" shipping entered the ports of Korea. Yet one of the first actions of the Department of State was to take all Army privileges away from the missionaries. If conditions had been normal, this could have been understood. But the act was indicative of the chasm that exists between the missionaries and our Department of State. Soon after AMIK became established, the missionaries lost PX, commissary, post office and transportation facilities. The only AMIK service that remained to them was the privilege of buying gasoline at the AMIK garage in Seoul. This last was a necessary exception, since all the gasoline in Korea was brought in by AMIK, and there were no authorized open-market sales of the precious liquid anywhere in the country.

It is curious that the American policy of nonservice to non-AMIK Americans did not extend to the diplomatic establishments of other nations in Korea. In spite of the fact that British shipping came into Inchon regularly, the members of the British consulate had full AMIK privileges, which were also extended to the staff of the United Nations Commission in Korea. The U. N. Commission had remained in Seoul to observe developments. In addition to its official membership from El Salvador, India, Turkey, France, etc., it employed a staff of clerks and typists (or précis writers, to use U.N. vocabulary). Every one of these men and women, regardless of rank or duties, enjoyed all the rights of the official American, while the American missionary fended for himself.

Not that the missionaries were unable to live without AMIK aid. Quick adjustments were made. Life was somewhat more complicated, but it went on. It is just that such unfairness only served to widen the gulf between men who were supposedly working for the same ends.

The impact of the Christian missionaries in Korea. in

China, in Japan, in all the Far East, has never been fully appreciated, even by the church people who support them at home. How much less has it been appreciated by our embassies, our officials, and our travelers abroad. It is sometimes necessary for us to realize that the Point Four program, ECA (now called Mutual Assistance), UNESCO, the State Department's information and cultural services, have all come on the scene in an attempt to improve the minds and bodies of "backward peoples," but that these programs are not new. The work of the missionaries had already advanced the Far East by at least half a century. These men and women sowed the seeds of democracy and Christian ideals which the Communists have been trying furiously to obliterate. For every Angus Ward of the State Department who has been seized and tried by the Communists, there have been a dozen Christian missionaries and priests who have suffered much more, who are in many cases still waiting in the lonely prisons of China and North Korea.

Since the 1880's, when the Underwoods and the Appenzellers arrived in Korea to begin their teaching, missionaries have been laying the groundwork for the adoption of Western standards of government, economy, and religion. By 1950 the physical evidence of their presence was staggering. From the Yalu River to Pusan could be found the hospitals, schools, colleges, universities, churches, and cathedrals built by their labors and the labors of their converts. In Seoul alone there were 290 Protestant churches, while in Pyongyang, capital of communist North Korea, there were once forty thousand Christians.

Over a century ago, Timothy Richards, a Baptist missionary in China, worked for flood control, public health, and improved transportation. A generation before the Wright brothers, he predicted that aviation would one day solve China's transportation problems. In 1885 he said that an exchange of students between nations would be one of the most far-reaching methods of developing international understanding and amity. Much of what he and other pioneer missionaries advocated has been included in the Point Four program which President Truman has called a "bold, new program." The exchange of students is now one of the State Department's proudest boasts, and rightly so. Yet of all our leaders in the Far East, past and present, only General Douglas MacArthur considered missionary work of crucial value to American prestige and position.

The westernization of the Far East would undoubtedly have occurred sooner or later even with no missionaries. It is only that the missionaries, dedicated to service in a way which our Foreign Service officers could well afford to emulate, have been ploughing the fields and fertilizing the soil of Asia to make our work that much easier, could we only take advantage of it.

In 1795, William Carey, one of the first Protestant missionaries to arrive in India, made himself felt throughout the land. He tells us that the words which took him so far from his native fields were those of the Old Testament: "Enlarge the place of thy tent . . . lengthen thy cords and strengthen thy stakes." He did just that. He was the first to advocate forest conservation and reforestation in India. He promoted the translation of the Indian classics into English, in the hope that the West might profit from reading the literature of the East, particularly that we might better grasp the oriental turn of mind. His work was decidedly the forerunner of our American cultural relations programs of today. His loud protests and authoritative studies sounded the death knell for the practice of infanticide in India.

The diplomats of those days were far from approving. Already the gap was forming between missionary and diplomat. The East India Company, representing as it did the British Crown in the eighteenth century, refused to let Carey work in territory controlled by the British. He was forced to set up his tent, which was to enlarge beyond expectation, in a city then under Danish rule. What Carey proposed in the way of enlightenment could jeopardize the existing rule and order which, to the East India Company, spelled profits.

During all my childhood I felt the difference between missionaries and the rest of the American community. Partly, perhaps, it was because we lived in somewhat less spectacular style. But also I could not help but pick up, from schoolmates in Shanghai as well as from some members of the family circle, some of the disapproval of missionary activities. I can remember one instance, many years ago, when my father, Harry R. Caldwell, was asked by the Chinese Government to act as a middleman, or mediator, between the government and the thousands of bandits who were at that time ranging the mountains of Fukien Province. The bandits were supplied with arms by the Japanese on nearby Formosa. My father had become famous as a killer of man-eating tigers. The Chinese Government trusted him; the bandits respected him for his tiger hunting exploits. But when the American consul in Foochow heard of the idea, he informed my father that if he accepted the proposal and meddled in the internal affairs of China, he would be deprived of all his rights as an American citizen.

Twenty-five years later, our Department of State took a somewhat different view when it sent General George Marshall to become quite a meddler in Chinese affairs—a meddling operation that has ended rather disastrously. Needless to say, my father went ahead, without protection or sanction of the consulate, and brought about peace in that time in Fukien. With the peace came an enormously increased respect for America, at a time when Western prestige was running dangerously low. It has been my observation that our Foreign Service officers have often done all they could to thwart men of action, and my father's experience would seem to be a case in point.

I have been speaking of the missionary work that contributed to a better physical life. I wonder, too, if there is not something of tremendous value to the conduct of our foreign relations, on the spiritual side of missionary teaching. There are in Asia few practicing Confucianists or Buddhists. The gods of Asia are gods of fear. The religion of the average Chinese or Korean is based upon an animism that creates fearsome devils of illness, drought, mountain, and river. Life is successful and happy only if a great succession of devils is somehow placated.

A religion of fear produces selfishness, greed, brutality, a fatalism that is hard to reconcile with progress. The religion of fear, added to continual economic stress, has created standards of morality quite different from those of the Western world. It may sound like old-time religion, but I wonder if we can ever expect full and proper use of American dollars and technical help as long as the people are in the grip of superstitious terror. Is it not actually necessary in a large measure to be "born again," to develop an entirely new thinking based upon a religion of love, a religion that emphasizes individual morality? It is certainly obvious by now that the Communists consider the work of missionaries a very grave danger to their cause. If the missionary and his work is considered so threatening by our enemy, might it not be wise for us to consider the value of the missionary as a member of our team?

Before liberation, the Korean's contact with Americans had been almost wholly limited to the missionaries, and the people were not well prepared for the behavior of American troops and officials. It was not a simple matter to reconcile the differences between missionary teachings (and example) and official American actions. The question of drinking itself —and I do not speak from a moral standpoint—was a serious difference not well understood by the AMIK official.

The devastating effects caused by indiscriminate drinking among the poor, encouraged by the Japanese in their systematic debauching of subject populations, had caused the missionaries to take a completely antialcoholic stand. Few people are more susceptible to the evil effects of liquor than are the Koreans, and the missionaries were strict in teaching against it—perhaps too strict. Into such a situation came young America, and the American Government, in force. I have already noted the fact that a great amount of our social life in Seoul was centered around the cocktail party. Much of the entertaining was quite expensive, money flowing where the Scotch flowed. The liquor bill of the American community ran as high as $40,000 a month, and the liquor was tax-free.

The missionaries in Korea tried constantly to point out what it was the Korean people most needed from us. According to men like Kris Jensen, Dr. Horace Underwood, Dr. William Shaw, and many others, what was needed was education in the simple skills and crafts and in agriculture. Democracy cannot be allowed, like Topsy, to just grow in a country like Korea. It must receive constant tutelage and guidance from men who are dedicated to their task.

The missionaries felt that some of our activities in Korea were not only expensive but of little practical value. Economic aid for such a country, they said, should be something the farmer and his children, the little shopkeeper in the crowded cities, could understand and play some part in. It should be something they could do to help themselves: Four-H clubs, for instance, many of which the missionaries had already organized, or the revival of ancient arts (ceramics, wood carving, weaving). It should be the kind of personal aid Samuel Gridley Howe once took to Greece.

Dams, power developments, mines, railways (the things that delight us) yes, all in good time, in proper proportion. Meanwhile, begin at the grass roots; and let the teaching be with love, or let's not have it at all. One cannot repeat too often that only a Christian can teach Christianity, only a cultured man can teach culture, only a democrat can prove that democracy works.

Korea has been fortunate in the missionaries that have devoted long and arduous years to its growth. There are half a dozen missionary dynasties, son or daughter following a father and grandfather, as in the case of the famous Underwood family in which a fourth generation is now growing up for service. Dr. and Mrs. Horace Grant Underwood, who herself was a medical doctor, were among the first Protestant missionaries to Korea. They entered Korea in the days when any Westerner was looked upon with the greatest suspicion, when Korea was truly the Hermit Kingdom. Mrs. Underwood was so successful in breaking down the walls of antagonism that she became physician to the royal family.

Dr. Horace Horton Underwood, their son, was the first white child born in Korea, to the best of my knowledge. He became one of Korea's great educators, following in his parents' footsteps. For years he was president of Chosun Christian College, which had been founded by his father and which is Korea's first and best institution of higher learning. It was his wife, some will perhaps recall, who was murdered by communist agents in the doorway of her home on the college campus in 1949. Her death was such a blow to her husband that ill health forced him to return to the States for a period of rest in 1950. When the invasion came, he tried in every way to return to his beloved foster land. The Army couldn't allow missionaries to go back as such, so Dr. Underwood volunteered for military service and returned in the fall of 1950. The strain of grief and overwork caused his death in February 1951.

At his deathbed there were three sons, the third generation of Korea Underwoods. Dick was in the U. S. Army, having volunteered from college directly after the invasion. John was an evangelistic missionary, a volunteer civilian interpreter with the Army. He had gone through the terrible battle for the Pusan perimeter, contributing all he could to the relief of the stricken population. And there was Horace, a lieutenant in the U. S. Navy, who had been teaching at Chosun Christian College at the time of the invasion but who volunteered the moment he was evacuated to Japan. Dr.

Underwood is buried in the little missionary cemetery in Pusan.

Through much of 1951 and 1952 Horace and Dick Underwood labored unheralded as principal United Nations interpreters at the Kaesong and Panmunjun truce tables. A third-generation missionary is bound to know the language and customs of the people his family has lived among. Horace and Dick had learned to think in Korean. This knowledge has been particularly important in the truce negotiations, where a shading of meaning can be of vital importance to the free world.

The Underwoods have been preaching missionaries, doctors, teachers, amateur scientists, and sailors. An inheritance from Uncle John, of the Underwood Typewriter Company, supplemented their modest missionary salaries, and it has been a family tradition to own a sailboat and to cruise the lovely Korean inlets along the wild coastline. Few if any Americans knew the approaches to Inchon, or the currents and mudbanks of the treacherous Han River, as did young Horace Underwood. As a result, he had an important part in planning the Inchon landing and was among the first Americans to step ashore that day. Acting as guide and interpreter, he was with the advance unit crossing the Han River in the first big battle for Seoul in September 1950 and led a small reconnaissance party which swam the river to probe enemy positions along the north bank. It is indeed sad that his mother, who had fallen in the same cause and on the same field, did not live to hear of the exploits of her son.

The Underwoods are far from being the only missionaries of note in Korea, nor were their sons the only missionary sons who rushed to the defense of the land of their adoption, the land for which they had endured so many hardships even in periods of peace. How tragic that a people as peace-loving by nature as the Koreans, whose language is full of such expressions as, "Are you in peace today?" or "Go in peace," should so often have been at war.

William (Bill) Shaw, son of a veteran Methodist missionary, was killed in action. He had been with Military Government, and later with AMIK, and had returned to the States
to complete his studies for missionary work, when the invasion came upon us. He volunteered immediately and was
quickly returned to Korea where he fell. His father, Dr.
William Shaw, is now a civilian chaplain, assigned to the
South Korean Army—the only Asiatic army which has ever
gone into the field with recognized chaplains.

There is Dr. Paul Crane, who developed in Chonju one of
the finest hospitals in the Orient and who tried hard to help
solve one of Korea's health problems by getting the posthole
latrine introduced. The British used this sanitation measure
to rid whole areas of India of intestinal parasites. It consisted
of drilling a hole for use as a latrine and of then sealing it
while a new hole was made elsewhere. After a period of
sealing, human waste is devoid of all parasites but can still
be used as fertilizer. Paul hoped to induce ECA to help in
his posthole program but without success.

Up in the mountains of Kangwon Province we had occasion to know another group of devout missionaries, the Catholic Columban Fathers, led by Monsignor Quinlan. He had
an invaluable knowledge of the country and its people, and
through him I learned a great deal of what was going on,
both north and south of the Parallel.

Monsignor Quinlan and his associates helped us in more
ways than one. For some reason, perhaps because there were
no Protestant missionaries in Chunchon, all Christian and
many non-Christian refugees from the North came first to
the Columban Mission. There they told their stories, and
Monsignor Quinlan mentally cataloged their skills and quali-
fications. Whenever any of us needed employees, we visited
the mission; or, as often as not, a Korean would appear at the
shrine with a note in the Monsignor's scrawl: "This man is
from the north. He is a good man if you need help." I soon
learned that these recommendations were foolproof, and that

they were given to Catholic, Protestant, and non-Christian alike without favor.

In return for the help Monsignor Quinlan gave our Military Government group, the group did something for him. Catholic and Protestant alike contributed generously to the new church he was building, and Battalion found an excuse to have bulldozers in the vicinity of the mission for several days while construction was going on. When we left Chunchon, the building was well on its way to completion.

There is Harold Voelkel, Presbyterian, a civilian chaplain, who is working in the communist prisoner camps on Koje Island; Francis Kinsler, again a Presbyterian, who is acting as an interpreter for the United Nations Commission in Korea; Dr. Howard Moffett, a young medical missionary, who has left his hospital in Taegu to serve as a surgeon in the United States Air Force; while Charles Bernheisel, son of pioneer missionaries, is an officer in the ground forces. A few of the younger missionaries have been called back to America, where they are taking one of the most intensive courses ever given on communism, a course sponsored by the churches and given at Union Theological Seminary in New York. It is the churches which have longest recognized the completely anti-Christian nature of the communist movement in Asia.

Our week ends at the beach gave us many opportunities to know the missionaries and their work, their hopes and aspirations for Korea. Only two weeks before the end of our Korea story, I sat on the porch of our cottage at Taechun and talked for hours with Kris Jensen of the Methodist Mission. Kris told me of his work in rural areas, a work that included, in addition to preaching, the initiation of chicken-raising projects in every village.

Many missionaries, like Kris, saw the need of material as well as spiritual development. These men and women realized that our task is one for spiritual and moral leadership, that real peace can only come by strengthening the moral fibre of a people, by setting an example of the stature we profess in our broadcasts, by showing the people of other nations that we ourselves seek greater compensations than materialism offers. Or, as David Lawrence puts it, war will be abolished "when people realize their true strength and assist each other in preventing the rise of dictatorships. . . . It calls for an understanding by peoples of their moral power even more than their material power. It calls for faith in the code of the Master and a willingness to apply it to ourselves as well as to others."

It would be foolish to assert that all of our missionaries were saints, that all of them accomplished wonders. Obviously, there were misfits, men so narrow that they did more harm than good. There were among the missionaries a few men who had little conception of the overall battle that was taking place in Korea.

Does all of this mean anything to us in our fight against communism? If we are honest we will admit that it has been the Christian converts who have offered the strongest resistance to communism both before and after the shooting war began. Though there has been very little guerilla resistance to communism north of the Parallel in Korea (this was eliminated by preventive medicine, so to speak, before it had opportunity to organize), that little has been led by Christians. There is one army of possibly three thousand young Christians which is said to be active in sabotage and guerilla attacks in the Pyongyang area.

South of the Parallel, in areas held by the United Nations, Christian leaders are trying to rally the stricken country. Hundreds of ministers are active in relief work. George Paik, former president of Chosun Christian College, has become Minister of Education, and in the face of incredible odds has kept most of the country's schools open—in rice fields, in creek beds, in bombed-out buildings.

The Communists reacted to the menace of Christianity in North Korea, just as in China, by systematically seeking to liquidate it. As early as 1950 they undertook that service in North Korea: 80 per cent of the Protestant clergy, and a larger percentage of the Catholic priests, were disposed of, often in ways too brutal to mention. Some Methodist and Presbyterian ministers were fortunate enough to escape, leading their flocks across the mountains into South Korea. Many of these were lost when the Communists took Seoul in June 1950. As in the case of Koreans who worked for Americans or had relatives in the United States, there were church and mission lists which proved an unfortunately effective help in liquidating them.

One of the great stories to come out of Korea since the war began is that of the refugee congregations which escaped from Hamhung and Pyongyang in North Korea to the safety of Pusan. On a hillside in Pusan today is a makeshift church with several hundred members known as the Pyongyang Church. At Christmas of 1951, the members of this church made an enormous Christmas offering. The money was to be used for the help of refugees, including non-Christians. A missionary questioned the minister about this surprising action and received the following explanation.

Just before Christmas the congregation had met to discuss what special Christmas offering could be made. It was pointed out that all of the membership had arrived in Pusan "by the grace of God, with no possessions except what could be carried." In the year that had passed, many of them had found jobs and places to live. A few were doing well. Since they had arrived with nothing a year before, and God had taken care of them, it was felt that the membership should have enough faith to start again from scratch. Each member gave all the money he had as of Christmas Day, putting himself back, as far as material things were concerned, to the day when he had arrived penniless and destitute after the long march south. I wonder if our own expression of faith might not give our millions of dollars in economic and technical aid a greater message of courage to the underprivileged of this earth who have such a long and desperate row to hoe before approaching our standard of living.

Unfortunately, American missionaries in Korea were allowed little part in the official American effort to build a republic on democratic principles. Instead of making good use of the foundations laid by missionary agriculturalists, doctors, and ministers, AMIK moved to one side, so to speak, and began building anew. Where missionaries had known the language for years, AMIK tackled the Korean problem minus the very words with which to discuss it with the people. In 1950, five years after driving the Japanese out of Korea, we attacked the language barrier, not by learning Korean, but by building an expensive edifice in one city to house a high-salaried faculty of eight fresh arrivals from the States who did not know Korean either. The invasion blew up the building, but not the idea. The English Teaching Institute was the Department of State's number one post-"war" project for Korea. A new building was prepared, the teachers were held on in Japan, and the project folded only because of the Chinese offensives of 1951.

The missionaries had educated their medical and agricultural experts in the peculiarities of Korean diseases, Korean soil and climate, and Korean superstitions. AMIK imported its theorists, to whom Korea had been a color on a map. The missionaries had won a hard-earned respect, making themselves inconspicuous among the poor, taking care not to break local customs, tolerating misdemeanors not too flagrant, but always setting a standard for Western morality. AMIK gave the people pause to wonder at, and then to imitate, the more glamorous sins.

As for the financial outlay, the total missionary expenditures in seventy-five years could scarcely begin to approximate the money spent by the U. S. Government in South Korea in a single year. One of the most persistent worries of American administrators in Korea was that American aid in the millions would have to be continued ad infinitum if

South Korea were to be kept alive. Perhaps it is an irrelevant comparison, but the Protestant churches in Korea (excluding the cost of upkeep for universities, hospitals, training schools) have long been autonomous and self supporting. The little churches in Chunchon, Kaesong, and Taejon paid their pastors not with American handouts but with money contributed by the memberships.

The early missionaries were able, and today are still able, to bring with them some things far less tangible than democracy. The Christian converts then and now face persecution and death. Nor did the Underwoods, the Jensens, the Shaws, and many others like them, work for money. They worked for an ideal. They gave service and brotherly love, and in so doing rendered double service. They made the name of America an honored one. Secondly, among the millions of Koreans and Chinese they have created for our country a vast reservoir of good will. Communism had scarcely been able to make an impression against us until it used guns.

There are two stories which should be read by Americans who train or study for work in our establishments abroad. Both stories are available in printed form. One tells of the beginnings of Methodist missionary work in Foochow, China, the city of my childhood. The other is the story of the senior Underwoods, and their work in nineteenth-century Korea. They are not only stories of spiritual victory. There were defeats, too. There were some among these pioneers who gave up, who, like American diplomats I have known, hated the country and the people, were critical of improper and inadequate housing, complained of the food. There was one Methodist missionary in Foochow who resigned in disgust because of what he termed "the double-dealing of the Chinese race." Others were made of sterner stuff. It needed stern stuff indeed, for it was *nine years and ten months* before the *first* convert came into the Church.

In spite of their failings and their failures, the missionaries did find a formula for building international understanding.

Until those who are responsible for our foreign relations realize the power of persons with this sort of integrity and
purpose, until they learn the lesson of men who work from
an individual standpoint rather than through the impersonal
voice of radio, the corrupted dollar, or the inhuman cata-
combs of an overstaffed bureaucracy, until then we are
bound to be caught short on sincere allies.

Our closer relations with the missionary community very
nearly led to a personal tragedy. Dr. Fletcher, Elsie's father,
in addition to being a physician and surgeon, was a good businessman. He had been in charge of the complicated business
procedures by which the Presbyterian Mission converted
dollars into *won*. If the official rate, upheld by ECA, had
been used, the dollars could not have supported the hospitals,
universities, and training schools. The Korean Government,
always appreciative of the missionary work, had agreed to
allow the mission to go into business. Dollars were used to
buy newsprint and cotton yarn. The goods were then sold,
with a resulting exchange at three or four times the official
rate. Dr. Fletcher had gone to America on furlough at a time
when tons of goods had arrived, and he entrusted to me the
job of selling the newsprint and yarn at the best possible
price.

My missionary business frequently took Elsie and me to
the Presbyterian Mission compound near Seoul's East Gate.
It was there, one afternoon, that Elsie was singled out for
attack by our enemies. She was walking down the driveway
from one house to another when a hidden assailant aimed
and fired. She fell, shot in the back. Fortunately the bullet
did not penetrate the spine.

In the days of fruitless police investigation that followed,
we often recalled what had happened to Mrs. Underwood
the year before. Our thoughts also turned back to Operation
Cigarette, to the threats we had received then, and to the
ambush on the Short Russia road. Apparently "they" had not
forgotten either. We did not know that within weeks they

would be on the march and would destroy in a matter of days almost all that had been done in South Korea. Somewhat bitterly, as I stood at Elsie's hospital bed, I remembered the words of caution when she was first assigned as my assistant at Peacock Mountain: "She is a good worker, but a missionary's daughter, and she is terribly anticommunist." However terrible the attempt on her life, it was a clear tribute to the things for which she stood.

Chapter 13

Seoul, June 25, 1950

SATURDAY, June 24, 1950, was the end of a typically busy week for the American colony in Seoul, Korea. The ordinary quiet had been broken by the just as ordinary excitements relative to a VIP in our midst; in this instance a *Very* Important Person: John Foster Dulles.

The American Embassy had arranged the usual trip to Uijongbu on the 38th Parallel, where Dulles had been photographed standing with South Korean officials and gazing out across no man's land. This was followed by the usual press conference, and the usual statement about America's interest in South Korea and the great progress being made by the South Korean Government. All the proper courtesies had been exchanged, and John Foster Dulles had left.

In the newspapers and the drawing-rooms of Seoul, another piece of news received almost as much attention as the more significant story of Mr. Dulles' coming and going. The story had broken of the high-ranking embassy official who had, it seems, been supporting the number one communist spy in South Korea. He had even supplied her with short-wave radio equipment, with which she had been able for months to send messages north! An American couple had expressed willingness to adopt the little towheaded "consequences" but we learned later that the North Koreans had interrupted that arrangement.

After several hours of torrential rains which had made the roads worse than usual, Saturday turned into a fine June day, warm and sunny. The weekly Northwest Airlines plane came in from the States shortly after noon, and many Americans were at Kimpo Airport to greet new arrivals and bid farewell to departing friends. Among the latter were Ralph and Sally Fisher, popular members of the colony, who were leaving for the States by way of Japan.

The *Reinholt*, a small Norwegian freighter, was reported at Inchon Harbor, 26 miles away—the only ship in harbor for some days.

At mid-afternoon there was a wedding at the Seoul Union Club. Two of the younger missionaries were married, and most of the missionary group within a large radius were in attendance, together with a few personal friends from the American Embassy. Immediately after the wedding, Kris Jensen, veteran Methodist missionary, left for a two-day trip to Kaesong, the large Methodist center on the Parallel north of Seoul. The very fine work being done there had been maintained courageously, in spite of the fact that parts of the city lay only a few hundred yards south of communist positions. The mission felt secure in its ability to evacuate in case of serious danger, since the embassy had notified it months previously that no real trouble was likely to arise, or that, at worst, there would be plenty of warning.

During the afternoon another large group of Americans (Presbyterian missionaries, including the Underwoods, and a handful of embassy families) had left Seoul Station in a special gasoline rail car, for Taechun Beach. The Presbyterians were to hold their annual meeting there, and many women and children had chosen this time to move to Taechun for the summer months. Since Taechun was without electricity, it had no radio or telephone communications with the outside world.

For the George Hopkinson family that Saturday was a day of worry. Hopkinson, financial expert for AMIK, had not been feeling well for several days. By Saturday afternoon he had taken a turn for the worse, and his wife had driven him out to the Seoul Sanitarium Hospital, seven miles east of the city. The doctors were mystified and advised him to remain for observation.

Out in the Sobingo area, on the banks of the Han River, there was the customary skeet and trap shoot. The Sobingo Gun Club was made up of officers attached to the Korean Military Advisory Group and civilians of the American Mission staff. A strong, friendly rivalry existed between military and civilian teams. The day was hot, and after the shoot many of us stopped by the KMAG pool or the pool at the transportation compound for a leisurely swim and a cold drink.

As usual, take any day of the year, the streets of Seoul, from Yung-dung-po to the North Gate, were crowded with Koreans. Among the thousands milling about, the talk was not of John Foster Dulles, or the 38th Parallel, or the departure of the Fishers, or the skeet shoot, or even of the Mata Hari from North Korea. It was concerned with the price of rice, and whether the monsoons would come in time to insure a good crop. The rice, already transplanted into the paddies, thirsted for rain. Prices, as always in June, were sky high and would only fall after the rains began. The people eyed the heavy clouds over North Mountain with hope, and prayer.

As the afternoon drew to a close the social life of the American colony increased in tempo. The usual big Saturday night dance was to be held at the palatial KMAG Officers' Club, and two large cocktail parties were to precede the dance—also as usual. Soon after dark the embassy bars at the Banto, Chisan, Naija and Traymore Hotels began to fill. In a dozen homes and private rooms the Saturday night poker games had started. The embassy taxi service was operating at capacity, shuttling men and women from hotel to hotel, to the bars, and to the private parties, dinners, and bridge games for the small fry who did not rank invitation to the bigger events. The activity and the interests duplicated those of any American colony from Pearl Harbor to Hong Kong,

Cairo to Capetown, on any Saturday night, past, present, and future.

True, here and there an American could be found who was interested in other pursuits than those indulged in by the majority of our two thousand nationals in Korea. On this particular Saturday, for instance, Marc Sherbacker had left by train for the temples and tombs of Kyungju, two hundred miles to the south. An ECA field party was on its way to the coal mines and power plant at Yongwol. Several parties were heading for Kangwha Island and other scenic spots in the vicinity of Seoul. But for most this Saturday night was spent as every other Saturday night had been spent for the past two years and more.

By four in the morning of Sunday, June 25, 1950, the last young couples were still lingering at the KMAG Officers' Club . . . the parties at the embassy bars had died or had moved to private quarters . . . George Hopkinson had taken a turn for the worse and his illness and been tentatively diagnosed as polio . . . the Northwest Airlines plane was just setting down at Shemya in the Aleutians as day was breaking . . . after a long and bumpy jeep ride, Kris Jensen had probably turned in for sleep in a house in the Methodist compound at Kaesong.

And, though none of us in Seoul were aware of it at the time, the communist armies had chosen 4:00 A.M. as the zero hour in which to pour across the 38th Parallel and launch their attacks at Kaesong and at Uijongbu, where Dulles had viewed naught but peace and quiet a few days before. Undoubtedly, the first moments of the invasion woke Kris Jensen and the five other missionaries at the Kaesong Methodist Mission, but we don't know how it fared with them. They have been swallowed up into the unknown and, except for a brief report over the communist radio nineteen months later, no word had been heard of them since Saturday, June 24.

The dark clouds over North Mountain had swung out

over the city at dawn, and there had been several hours more of heavy rain, good to sleep by and cooling, a blessing on the land. The price of rice in the morning markets would take a drop. The people woke on a wave of relief and expectation. I was one of them.

I went into our garden about nine and was joined by our "outside man," Chi-se-bang. We stood and talked, gloating over the rainfall and, like the earth, absorbing the longed-for damp. Suddenly a powerful plane flew low, but still invisible, through the clouds above us, and I wondered idly whether Northwest Airlines had a special flight coming into Kimpo.

Toward noon Jack Thorne and his wife dropped in to take a look at some of my pottery and porcelain. We had cakes and coffee. I was trying to persuade the Thornes to accompany us to Kaesong next day to see the kilns where the ceramics were being made for export, when the telephone rang.

It was John Baldridge, who lived a couple of blocks below us in the transportation compound. His words made no sense. He was asking whether my wife and I would like to join his family in an attempt to get south to Pusan by car—right away, before it was too late. In my ignorance, I must have sounded as mad to him as he sounded to me. The Communists, he said, had begun a full-scale attack several hours ago, had already taken Kaesong, and were pushing across the Imjin River and into the Uijongbu corridor, spearheading for Seoul. As it turned out, it took them no more than sixty hours to reach this objective, sixty hours that no American or Korean that stood in their path will ever forget.

Yet, for many of those hours, nothing but optimism prevailed among the Koreans, and optimism was also the official tone of the American Embassy. Not that the possibility of a communist attack had never been considered (an elaborate evacuation plan, *in vacuo* and classified top secret, had been in the files since '48), but the possibility had long since been a joking matter. It was common knowledge in Seoul that the embassy, and therefore the United States, considered communist morale low, their military equipment poor, their aims not too inimical to ours.

Just three weeks before, *Time* (to all other nations the official news organ of the States) in no uncertain terms told of the embassy's splendid work in training the South Korean Army. General William Roberts was quoted as saying that the South Koreans had "the best damn army outside the United States." And everyone knew that Harold Noble, First Secretary of the American Embassy, had stated publicly that the South Korean Army could not only stop an attack but could move north and take over the communist capital in two weeks' time.

Through the Voice of America the South Korean people had been assured, again and again, that the U. S. Government had been delivering enormous amounts of military equipment. Yes, according to Noble, and Jim Stewart, and Lt. Col. Vanderpool (the embassy's Seoul-bound intelligence experts) the South Korean Army had reached such a high pitch of training and arming that an attack on the North was more to be feared than one from the North.

What wonder, then, that the Koreans were not greatly disturbed, that they had entire faith in American aid and in their own army, and that even our American colony failed to respond to the menace of approaching events. It was not until four o'clock Sunday afternoon that Ambassador John Muccio made his first public statement, broadcast over WVTP, the embassy's radio station. He told us there was no reason to be concerned, the South Korean Army had already contained the attack. (There had as yet been practically no contact between the two forces, and the North Korean tanks were advancing at will.)

The spirits of the Koreans rose to a patriotic fervor as their troops began to move rapidly and fearlessly north, passing through Seoul in a steady stream of trains, trucks, jeeps, bicycles and oxcarts (the lack of tank support somehow going unnoticed). Every truckload was wildly cheered by the vast crowds that thronged every downtown street. Monsoons, the price of rice, were forgotten. There was a sense of relief in the air, like a great sigh when a burden of suppression and strain has been lifted. After five sad years of an unrealistic and unsupportable division of a people, unification of their country seemed just over the horizon. There was not the slightest doubt in the minds of all that victory was theirs, and soon. I spent several hours during the day down on the street in front of the Severance Hospital compound, watching the troops move forward, singing, and while they passed the crowds cheered. I could not help a lump in my throat; all differences seemed to have been forgotten; white-clad farmer and businessman dressed Western style, both stood together behind their army.

Yet within a few hours the news we picked up over the U. S. Armed Forces Radio in Los Angeles startled us with an entirely different and more ominous story. When Yak fighter planes began to appear over the city, even bombing and strafing Kimpo Airport, something whispered in our hearts that the future was not going to be altogether rosy. Shortly after the Kimpo attack I called a high embassy official for news of events and plans. In looking back, his comment on events is rather amusing. "John," he said, "this thing is serious. They strafed an American plane. That's destruction of American property!"

John Baldridge and some others were among the first to take the hint. At least they began to pack. Friends in the Military Advisory Group said that the military analysis of the situation was in clear disagreement with that of the diplomatic. Consequently, a tug of war was under way at the embassy between those who advised an immediate evacuation of women and children, and the ambassador, who did not believe that an evacuation was necessary or advisable. The mounting roar of artillery seemed to add support to the contentions of the less optimistic group.

The argument raged throughout the day and far into the night. At midnight the ambassador finally yielded but insisted that the original evacuation plans which called for an airlift be abandoned. He did not wish to chance an international incident, what with the communist and American planes both in the air at once. The air plan was scrapped in favor of sending *six hundred and eighty-two* women and children out by way of the little Norwegian ship at Inchon, a freighter having a full cargo of fertilizer and accommodations for *twelve* passengers.

It is difficult at this late date to penetrate the veil of secrecy that the Department of State has thrown around the confused incidents of June 25, 26, and 27 and reveal the truth of what did occur. There are those who say that Ambassador Muccio was to the last ditch against leaving Seoul, who quote him as saying that even if the Communists did succeed in taking the city there need be no great alarm since diplomats would be treated as diplomats according to the laws of civilized nations. Yet, when we did evacuate, our exodus was so hasty and chaotic, so awkward and confused, that no effort was made to salvage or give to the Korean Army the fifteen hundred American vehicles in Seoul. (The only vehicles saved were those attached to the embassy fire department, and this because the Korean firemen took matters into their own hands and drove them three hundred miles south to safety.) Twenty-two thousand gallons of gasoline were left in the embassy motor pool. A hundred thousand dollars worth of food was abandoned in the embassy commissary. Forty thousand dollars worth of liquor (the July quota!) had just arrived and remained in the embassy bars and the embassy liquor store. Lost personal effects have been valued at $4,500,000, and claims totaling this amount are now before Congress.

Most terrible of all, most heart-rending, we left behind as we fled precipitately in the gray dawn of Tuesday morning, June 27, five thousand South Korean employees of the embassy, *with their personnel records left untouched*. We had destroyed our own confidential papers in a huge bonfire, but somehow the dossiers of our faithful workers had been overlooked and remained to be used as a ready-made list for persecution and execution. The persecution began on Wednesday, the 28th, and continued through the summer months of 1950. The number of drivers, houseboys, translators, interpreters, secretaries, who have been killed will never be known, or where and how they perished. They have disappeared into the unknown that also swallowed Kris Jensen, Bishop Cooper, Commissioner Lord of the Salvation Army, Vyvyan Holt (the British Ambassador who stayed on after the city fell in the mistaken belief that his country's recognition of Chinese communism would give him immunity), and hundreds of Methodist and Presbyterian ministers and church workers.

After it was all over and we had come away, Ambassador Muccio proudly announced the evacuation of 2,200 American citizens without a fatality or even, as he said, "a bloody nose." He returned to Washington to be honored by our government.

It was, as I have said, late Sunday night when the ambassador was persuaded that British and American women and children should leave immediately. It was then we learned that the British had warned their citizens of a possible evacuation three weeks before. The British had a total staff of six in Seoul, but had been able to read the signs.

At 11:00 P.M. radio station WVTP ordered all dependent women and children, and others who wished to leave, to assemble at certain points by three in the morning for transport by bus, truck, and car to Inchon and departure on the *Reinholt*. Since by good fortune Elsie was still an employee of the United States Information Service in Korea, she was able to remain behind with me. She was thus spared the fearful three-day sea passage to Japan, where fifty were removed to hospitals by stretcher, one child down with smallpox, thirty with dysentery, and no one having escaped the illness and suffering due to the odors of commercial fertilizer, lack of space, lack of hot food, lack of proper clothing. What would have happened in case of storm or enemy attack does not bear consideration.

By now of course, sleep was impossible for anyone. Elsie and I tried sorting our belongings: what we had to take, what we wanted to take, what we couldn't take. At the embassy later we saw our fellow refugees leaving with so little, and that of the strangest selection! One woman carried only her cocker spaniel; another carried two antique vases. The cocker reminded me of our two dogs, and I wondered whether it would be more merciful to shoot them before I left. It ended by our giving the dogs to our yardman's safekeeping. We have heard since of the clubbing to death of Blackie, my bird dog, to serve as food for the communist soldiers garrisoned in our compound. During the day we made one more trip to the information center to see old friends for the last time: Hong Shin, Cooper Kim, Slim Kim, and all the others who had worked with us long and faithfully. The good-byes were unspoken, for optimism was still in the air as far as the Koreans were concerned.

At three o'clock Monday morning the young embassy doctor called and asked me to make arrangements at Severance Hospital for George Hopkinson to be moved there. Communist tanks were approaching Seoul Sanitarium Hospital, and all patients were being evacuated. I was told George was very ill. He was brought into our compound near dawn, but too late to see his wife and little boy, who were already on their way to Inchon.

Meanwhile, the hundred-odd missionaries at Taechun Beach had been forgotten in the confusion and uncertainty. I had called the embassy before daylight Monday morning, reminding it that the group at Taechun included over a hundred Americans. Since there was no method of communication, Frank Barnhardt, son of a missionary and an official of the embassy, set out to drive the 135 miles over the narrow mountain roads. We heard afterward that he made the distance in five hours, organized a convoy of the few available vehicles, and led it south and east towards Pusan. It was a desperate journey for all concerned.

When the group reached Taejon, still one hundred miles from the front, it had planned to go on by morning train. But so confused had our officials become that the group was advised by radio to keep going. The local KMAG unit was ordered to destroy its communications system at once. All the Americans fled south by truck. Such haste and consequent loss of property turned out to be unnecessary. The battle of Taejon was not to start for another three weeks.

By mid-afternoon on Monday the roar of artillery was loud and incessant. Planes, enemy planes, were everywhere overhead. Since the Korean Air Force consisted of some twenty American light trainers, the Communists had little opposition. But when I talked to Jim Stewart at four that afternoon he assured me the tide had turned, and that the *Reinholt*, which had finally weighed anchor an hour or so before, after herculean endeavors on the part of Ralph Bricker, would probably be recalled.

Returning from Inchon, Bricker begged the ambassador to order the packing of embassy equipment, personal and official, to be sent south by train and truck. By putting to work every member of the staff, American and Korean, Bricker said we could have all movable equipment rolling out of Seoul by Tuesday morning. His suggestion was overruled. The embassy would be open for business as usual, and any talk of a mass withdrawal was to cease: it would affect morale adversely.

Seven or eight hours later, the "poorly equipped and trained communist armies" were ten miles from Seoul, and "the best damn army in the world outside the U.S." was retreating in utter chaos, streaming across the Han River in a demoralized route. Since the ambassador, following our precedent in China, did not believe the American staff was supposed to actually help the Koreans fight, there was a great confusion as to what our five hundred military advisors were expected to do. By midnight Monday the situation was declared hopeless, KMAG communications as far as two hundred miles behind the front were ordered destroyed, and all officers and men were ordered to seek safety. We ourselves were advised from Japan that planes would be arriving at daylight to begin the evacuation by air of all Americans remaining in Seoul. General Douglas MacArthur in Japan had finally put an end to the embassy's dilemma by telling us what to do.

At 3:00 A.M. an official of the embassy began to read the long list of names of those who were to board the buses for Kimpo. George Hopkinson's name was not on it. I tried to interest someone in having him taken to Kimpo on a stretcher. There was no time for such an arrangement. True, it probably would not have helped, since George was near the end with polio. He died alone at Severance Hospital just as the last buses were pulling out from Seoul. Two Korean doctors came to the embassy for burial instructions. At that moment the American flag was being lowered and the key turned in the front door. There was no one left to give instructions. The Koreans took George out to a little cemetery on the edge of town where he was buried.

On a hillside at the edge of town an execution was taking place. The Korean Mata Hari, mistress of the American official, met her death at the hands of a South Korean firing squad just as the communist tanks began to roll into Seoul.

In New York, Korean members of the Voice of America, the men and women who had been broadcasting words of faith and encouragement to their people as the official voice of our government, read the news from Korea with growing fear. They had relatives and friends in Seoul. These relatives and friends would be marked for death when the communist armies seized the city. On Sunday morning, Washington time, one of the New York Korean personnel telephoned the Department of State in Washington asking the department to cable the Seoul embassy in the hope of locating and assisting his wife and children. The official in Washington was curt and final. The department, he said, did not consider the matter or the situation of sufficient importance to warrant a cable, but it would be glad to write Ambassador Muccio.

During the days that followed there were incidents of heroism, treachery, and tragedy in Seoul.

There was the ECA official who returned to Seoul, late Tuesday, dog-tired from a long jeep ride. Without knowledge of Korean, he did not know what had happened and went to bed in his hotel. He has not been heard from since.

There were Koreans who began to steal American property before the last American was out of sight. There were other Koreans who took the possessions of their American employers and lovingly concealed them, to triumphantly bring them out of hiding months later.

There was the story of Fat Chai, the Korean Chief of Staff, darling of the cocktail set, who lost his head and blew up the Han River bridge with hundreds of his troops crossing it.

There were thousands of South Korean soldiers who fled without firing a shot; there were other hundreds who bravely attacked Russian tanks with bazookas which merely bounced off the steel armor.

There were Koreans, once trusted by the Americans, who turned out to be communist cell leaders; there were hundreds of Koreans who fled rather than live a day under communist rule.

Down at Inchon, Mrs. David Ahn, wife of the Korean manager of the United States Information Service, watched with alarm as the American women and children left. Her husband, David, was in America on a State Department grant. David had been outstandingly anticommunist, and working for the U. S. Information Service put him and his family high on any communist list. As had been the case with the other USIS offices scattered over Korea, no one had given any instructions, and the June salaries, due to be paid the last few days of the month, had been forgotten in the mad rush. Mrs. Ahn was not an American citizen, so she could not get passage on the *Reinholt* or even on the *Flying Snapper*, an American ship which came briefly into port after the *Reinholt* weighed anchor.

By Tuesday night the guns were close to Inchon and Mrs. Ahn's predicament was desperate. Her home was high on the hillsides overlooking the harbor. And in the harbor, lying forgotten on the mud, was the *S. S. Judge Medina*. Mrs. Ahn remembered the *Judge* in her hour of need. With communist troops just outside the city, she rounded up the crew and the Korean staff of the information center. They scrambled aboard and set out to sea. As I have said previously, the *Judge* was not made for deep-sea voyaging. She shipped water at the slightest provocation. For days the refugees cruised about, ever fearful of communist patrol boats, until a passing Chinese freighter picked them up and carried them to safety in Formosa.

None of us knew, in those last days of June, of the real tragedy ahead. For twenty million Koreans the months that have passed have meant almost unbelievable suffering. Every city from the Yalu River south for five hundred miles has been destroyed. Vast refugee camps dot the southern coast. Thousands of orphaned children wander the land. On one winter's day a hundred and some babies were born in a single camp, to join the suffering millions or shortly die.

Grave registration teams of the United States scour the hills and valleys, searching for bodies of Americans, French, Turks, Greeks, in order to ascertain whether the terrible words "missing in action" should be changed to the hopeless "killed in action." From the North come lists of prisoners. Now and then an escaped prisoner stumbles across the Parallel.

For many of us Americans who lived through those days,

it was a tragedy of a different sort. We lost our belongings and many of our friends, but our greatest tragedy was the end of a dream we had a part in building. We had been through the muddles of the American Occupation, had taken a part in the first free and democratic election in a nation's history. We had seen the new government emerge, with all its inexperience, selfishness, graft, and corruption, into the beginnings of real independence for a people who had sought independence for centuries. We had seen the valiant efforts of some Americans, the mistakes and avarice of others, all of them having a share in realizing the dream. But for all of us, missionary, diplomat, and common man, it ended on that Sunday, June 25, 1950.

Here in America men and women have differing opinions of the ultimate solution, of methods to prevent more Sundays in June in other parts of the world. There are those who rely on the power and materialism of the atomic bomb; those who seek to solve our problems by appropriating more and more money, hiring more and more people; there are those who advocate turning away from the world and its confused misery.

Before reaching a final decision we might well heed a Korean proverb which says, "When a man slips and falls into the stream, it is foolish to blame the stream."

THE END

INDEX